FAIRWAYS

The mature beginner's
short cut to golfing heaven

By

Andrew Simpson

By the same author:

REBECCA THE LURCHER
SUMMER PUDDING
GOSPEL TRUTH?

Fairways
written and published by Andrew Simpson
Fox Twitchen, East Kennett,
Marlborough, Wilts SN8 4EY
(01672) 861122
abridger.simpson@lineone.net

NOTES

NOTES

FAIRWAYS

The mature beginner's
short cut to golfing heaven

Andrew Simpson

CONTENTS

Introduction pp. 1 - 3

INTRODUCTION

The trouble with golf is the amount there is to learn. Quite apart from aiming at a hole, swinging a club and hitting a ball, there are a thousand gremlins that lurk in the shadows until the moment comes for one or other of them to emerge and bite the novice on the ankle. These gremlins do not feature in the lessons given by club professionals. They are simply facts of life which will make a difference and which have to be discovered by trial and error, over a period of time.

In most games, the equipment is limited: a bat, a ball, a pair of shoes, and off you go. In golf, your bag is overflowing with a multitude of devices which may or may not be required, depending on ever-changing circumstances, and you are expected to be in complete control of their infinite variety at every stage.

In most games, if you hit the ball into the stands, someone throws it back onto the pitch. In golf, the stands become part of the pitch and you play your next shot from in among a row of tip-up seats. That's poetic licence, but the principle is sound: in golf you never know where your next shot is going to take you.

Four hours out on the course. What about the weather, and how do you react when it changes? And then changes back again?

Four hours? What about your stomach? Your digestion? Your bladder? What about the blood when you impale your finger on the pitchmark repairer as you snatch for a tee in the depths of a pocket? The game goes on and you must do the best you can under all circumstances - and this has only been a thumbnail sketch of the trials and tribulations, which to a great extent have nothing to do with the art of swinging a club and aiming.

Those who start as children have generally learned to handle these potential hazards by the age of twenty, teenage beginners reach enlightenment by thirty, and those who take up the game at twenty-five achieve competence at about forty.

The only people who have a real problem are those who take up the game at about the age of retirement. At this stage The Grim Reaper is not yet calling the shots, but one thing is for certain: no mature novice can afford to spend fifteen years picking up the tricks of the trade.

Hence this booklet. I reckon that with its assistance the essential tricks can be assimilated in two years instead of fifteen, during the period when the novice is getting to grips with the basics of aiming, swinging and hitting. At the end of that time, I am confident that you will be well qualified to deal with most of those gremlins lurking in the shadows.

What more could the mature beginner ask for?

Good luck.

Chapter 1

WHY GOLF?

Why golf? You've taken early retirement, and the love of your life doesn't want you under her feet all day. Or his feet, depending on which of you is reading this. You need to get out of the house – for several hours at a time. Wouldn't it be convenient if you could slope off, with your old bag on your shoulder... I'll re-phrase that... with your golf bag on your shoulder, a gleam in your eye and a song in your heart? "See you teatime, darling!" Golf is a most effective insurance against domestic violence.

Why golf? The kids have left home. An empty house is getting on your nerves. Instead of kicking the cat, hit a ball.

Why golf? You're fifty-two, and have had your first heart attack. The doctor recommends healthy exercise, nothing too violent, and tells you not to worry – he's probably right on all three counts.

How good is the exercise which golf provides? I was in the habit of jogging pretty regularly throughout my forties and into my fifties. When I took up golf, the jogging was more or less shelved, and the golf that replaced it usually consisted of nine holes (walking about two miles) three or four times a week.

On two occasions I remember going out for a jog after not having done so for several months. Each time I cautioned myself against doing too much after such a long lay-off, and on both occasions I covered two and a half miles with ease – no puffing, no soreness, could have doubled the distance without any effort, and no adverse after-effects. So I was comparatively fit – thanks to just nine holes, three or four times a week. That's not bad.

Why golf? Fresh air. Trees, leaves in autumn. Birdsong. Mown grass. Rabbits, hares, pheasants, the occasional deer, a kestrel hovering – so much to admire and enjoy. Getting soaked and then frozen makes one really appreciate hot water, makes food and drink taste better, sometimes even makes one sleep like a baby. All this, plus the chance to leave the mobile at home and enjoy true freedom.

Why golf? Man is a social animal – golf is a social game - be social. In addition, you will learn more about other people in a few hours on the golf course – for better or for worse - than in several years in any other environment (apart from a war, I imagine). It's very interesting, and often useful in more ways than you might expect.

Why golf? You are no longer a callow young thing. You have more cunning, more patience, more self-control than you had earlier in your life. There are less distractions since you gave up football/netball – even less if you have retired from business, and/or have given up chasing men/women. You are ideally qualified to become, not just a golfer, but a competent golfer for all these reasons.

Why golf? I haven't even mentioned the fact that golf is an immensely difficult game to play well, and that setting about that formidable task is an effort which will do you nothing but good. Just putting one's shoulder to the wheel is enough to banish any suggestion that one is over the hill.

In addition, the ups and downs with which the game bombards the player are extremely good for the character. It is almost certainly true that an industrious golfer will eventually be shown to one of the better seats in Paradise. Some claim that Paradise is in fact a golf course.

Chapter 2

HOW DO YOU START?
Part 1

How do you start? First sit down in front of the television, and watch professional golf. Have a glass of beer or a whisky and something at your elbow. Do this more than once, over a period of time. Just sit there and soak it all up (especially the professional golf).

After about twenty-five minutes, you will have noticed that nobody does anything very explosive, or muscular or violent. All you will have seen is a series of long, slow, elegant movements, performed by players of all shapes and sizes, who comfortably maintain perfect balance at every stage of the proceedings. A thing of beauty, rather than a display of brute strength.

In those twenty-five minutes you will have digested one of the fundamentals of playing the game more or less properly: jabbing, stabbing, heaving, straining, exploding, contorting, falling about – none of these has a place in golf as it is played by those who play it properly.

Once you know that, you know enough to separate you from the idiots. In your quest for improvement on the golf course, if ever you find yourself jabbing, stabbing, heaving, straining, exploding, contorting or falling about, you will immediately realise that you have strayed from the path of enlightenment, and that the pain you are suffering (people who jab and stab always suffer) is the result of a simple mistake which can be put right in an instant.

How? Just stop, and spend a little time reminding yourself that the name of the game is "long, slow, elegant, balanced and comfortable." You know that that is so, because you have seen it with your own eyes, and it works.

It is also a very good thing for men (as well as women) to watch the top women golfers. This is particularly appropriate for people taking up golf when past the first bloom of youth. They will find that most of the women are slim, shapely, ethereal creatures, and as a general rule not especially weighty or muscular. Their ability to hit the ball extremely well is just one more indication that skill and timing, rather than power, are the keys to success. So we seniors can take heart: age is no barrier to skill or to timing.

Chapter 3

HOW DO YOU START?
Part 2

The beginning of the adventure may well be fortuitous. A casual drink in a strange pub, a conversation at a party, a program on TV, a walk with the dog, a doctor's word of warning – or a booklet like this one. Any one of these could lead to a phone call or two, the picking of several brains, and an outing during which three dervishes convince one seeker-after-enlightenment of the superiority of their particular religion, punctuating each philosophic thrust with a flourish and a ping, and a little white ball more or less soaring into the wide blue yonder, proclaiming the wonders of the great god Golf.

My introduction was the result of a dinner party (and overnight stay) to celebrate a crossword puzzle contest, in which I won a prize. The following morning I found myself, painfully hung-over, ill-shod in paper-thin shoes, splashing round a semi-flooded three-hole practice golf course.

I swung a five-iron (not that I would have known a five-iron from a policeman's helmet at that stage), made contact with the ball and watched it soar away, higher and higher, further and further, in just about the intended direction. I was hooked.

If something similar happens to you, by all means let the thing develop as fortuitously as seems good to the mysterious forces which control our destiny, but never forget that you will be better off with a Plan, a Structure, a Strategy. Not because you are some kind of frustrated militarist. Simply because you are no longer in the first flush of youth, and cannot afford the luxury of wasting time by stumbling down a succession of blind alleys.

Of what should this Strategy, this Structure, this Plan consist?

You must make sense of the following: Clubs (the institutions), Teachers, Clubs (the implements), Practice, more Practice, and Games, in roughly that order.

Success or failure will depend on how you juggle these balls in the air over a period of, to start with, six months. At the end of that period, if you do things right, you will find yourself on a mountain-top, gazing down upon the Promised Land, and rubbing your hands in gleeful anticipation. If you do things wrong – but that's not going to happen, is it?

Chapter 4

CLUBS, TEACHERS, AND MORE CLUBS

Clubs (the establishments)

In the western world, especially in Great Britain, you will be surrounded by golf clubs. Let your friends take you to several, visit others on your own, get a feel about which factors are important to you (location, facilities, costs, atmosphere, reputation of the teaching professionals, etc.), and don't be in a hurry to join. In Britain, with the present state of the market (too many clubs for too few players), you will be welcome to play as a guest of a member, or as a visitor, without anybody pressing you to join – not at first, anyway. Apart from anything else, visitors, paying green fees each time they visit, provide an extra source of revenue for the club, which is much needed and much appreciated. So spread the net, and in due course you will find a club which suits you down to the ground.

Apply, get yourself proposed and seconded, join the waiting list if there is one, and continue playing as a "guest" or "visitor" while you wait for your membership to be processed.

Does one have to be very, very civilised to be a member of a golf club? Forget the "very, very" – just plain "civilised" will do. How does one know whether one is in fact civilised? If in doubt, take a chance on it. You'll probably be perfectly all right. The fact that you are drawn to golf is in itself an indication of high-mindedness.

However, if in the fullness of time it turns out that you cheat, get falling-down-drunk in the bar on a regular basis, and can't stop pawing the lady captain's upper body, the outraged members will unquestionably rise up against you and you will be consigned to the outer darkness, indicating a "less-than-civilised" rating on your scorecard. And who can blame them?

Teachers

Every club will have one or more teaching professionals. In the ideal world, the club you join will have the teacher you want to learn from, and it is reassuring to know that the vast majority of club pros are eminently capable of getting the average beginner off to a good start. This is because the game's governing bodies have established a system whereby aspiring pros are well trained and rigorously tested before being licensed.

However, in golf, as in every other cultural activity, really good teachers are few and far between, and the novice will be hugely advantaged if he can learn the game from the best available. Listen to what more experienced players have to say about the quality of tuition available in your area.

The ideal is to have a good relationship with your own club professional, who sees more of your strengths and weaknesses than anyone else, while at the same time feeling free to seek enlightenment elsewhere, if the need arises, or if the whim takes hold of you. Most professionals are allowed to teach people who are not members of their club, and it is generally accepted that members are free to spread the net in their search for perfection.

The absence of restrictive practices is a refreshing indication of the civilised attitudes of the golfing world. On the other hand, the novice must be careful: more than one teacher at any one time – that way madness lies.

When you begin, it might be sensible to have an intense week of lessons, followed by something like one a week for six weeks. During those first weeks you can play games, practice on your own, get into strange and impossible predicaments, climb to the peaks of euphoria and sink to the depths of despair, secure in the knowledge that at your next lesson much will be explained, and all will turn out for the best.

In the longer term, a refresher course at regular intervals is not a bad idea. For example an annual golfing MOT could feature in your diary, to make sure that the machinery is sound enough to see you through another year.

Let us not forget that human nature is far from perfect. In golf it betrays us, by allowing malign deviations to transform one's technique without one having the slightest idea that a deviation has developed.

But the pro takes one look and is horrified. "Why are you doing such, and such, and such – when I told you a year ago to do this, and that, and thus!"

You gasp like a fish out of water, you promise not to fall from grace ever again – but be warned, one needs eternal vigilance (and the help of one's betters) to avoid the recurring pitfall.

In addition, as you get more confident, and maybe more competent, you may well set your sights higher and higher and yearn for the ability to do quite difficult things with club and ball. At such times, words of wisdom and a guiding hand will be worth more than rubies.

<u>Clubs (the implements)</u>

I bought my first set of clubs on my own at an auction of household goods. I flailed away with them for some time without making any progress before consulting my club pro.

He took one look and said, "Those were made twenty years ago. They are called 'blades' and were designed for extremely good players only. You are like a learner driver let loose in a very old Formula One car. Disaster is inevitable."

"What should I be using?"

He indicated the massed ranks of clubs in his shop. "You want a fairly cheap set of clubs designed by a reputable firm specifically for beginners. Among other things, they have a large 'sweet spot', which improves the player's chance of making good contact with the ball. When you have mastered the basics of the game, you could consider moving on to clubs that are more ambitious."

He sold me a set of clubs, and the difference they made was remarkable. You see, worth more than rubies!

Chapter 5

PRACTICE

1: Practice at home

If you have no space at home where you can practice, it's not the end of the world. But if you do have space, so much the better. It is such an advantage to have clubs in one's hands every day. Just a few minutes can make a difference.

My garden is just long enough for me to practice chips and pitches fairly satisfactorily. I always hit balls away from the house. Windows are so, so fragile. With grass of the right length and density it is even possible to practice bunker shots, and I found it quite easy to develop a patch of deep jungle to practice getting out of the rough.

For practising longer shots, I use the practice balls which look like ping-pong balls with holes in them. They only go about twenty yards. Take note: that is as far as they are meant to go. Don't try to make them go further by hitting them harder and harder. You'll start doing bad, bad things. Just swing through them nicely, like Justin Rose.

You might invest in a net, into which you can hit proper golf balls as hard as you like. However, I have reservations about nets, which I reveal later on.

I don't have any grass that is suitable for putting, so I do it indoors, on a carpet. One has to remember that the speed on carpet will be different from grass. Even so, you can use it to sharpen up your aim. Let your targets be chair legs – which give you much less to aim at than a proper hole on a proper green. After chair legs, the real thing is child's play ((Don't believe a word of it).

[Two years later: I have given up putting on carpet. The surface is so different from grass that, in my experience, it does more harm than good.]

Padraig Harrington, winner of two of the four Major titles in 2008, said, "Beware, practice makes permanent." It's true, so only practice things which you know are correct. Otherwise you will spend hours and hours innocently and unwittingly acquiring bad habits, which will take an age to unlearn.

Likewise, make certain that when you practice you are concentrating fully, and stop before your attention-span is exhausted. Take the word of one who has fallen into the trap and paid the price - practising when you don't really feel like it makes you casual. When you're casual you play bad shots. Result – you get worse instead of better.

Is "Operation Golf" beginning to sound hideously difficult? So it should – all the experts rate it the most difficult game in the world. Don't be frightened. Be proud that you have dared to take on such a formidable challenge.

2: Practice at the club

All clubs have a practice facility.
Where I play there is an area where you can chip on
to a choice of three greens either off grass or out of
a bunker.

There is also a green for putting practice only.

There is also a caged net, where one can hit balls to
one's heart's content without spraying them all over
the place. A word of warning: in a net your ball
only travels ten or twelve feet before the net catches
it. Consequently the player can be tempted to hit
much too hard, because he has no idea whether his
shots would have become horrible slices or vile
hooks if they had been allowed "free range". So use
the net for basic rhythm and timing and balance and
good contact, rather than for power.

Finally there is a practice range where you can hit
shots of any distance up to about 250 yards. There
are flags at various intermediate distances, so one
has every opportunity to go through all one's clubs.

I visit one or other part of the practice area several times per week, and I love it. Be careful, however. the temptation to hit balls like a machine gun should be resisted. When you are playing golf "for real," you don't have the chance to hit four or five balls towards the target, nor is there the possibility of congratulating oneself if three out of five go close. When it is your shot in a real game, you have one chance and one chance only. Your attitude in practice should reflect this harsh reality. You should be slow and deliberate and make each shot the most important thing in your life at that particular moment.

That may sound a bit over the top, but it isn't. If you are standing over a ball, with a club in your hand, and you are going to hit that ball with that club, with a view to moving it from A to B via a chosen trajectory, how can anything else be more important during the time it takes to do the job in hand?

Between shots, of course you can turn your attention to the mortgage, or the war in Iraq, or the state of the roads, but not while you are planning and playing the shot. That's just common sense.

Concentrate, and as soon as you feel that your concentration is wilting, pack in the practice.

Now here's a thing that has always intrigued me. Most of the people I play with tend to meet on the first tee at the time arranged, but very few of them spend ten or twenty minutes beforehand on the practice ground. As a result it takes them four or five holes to warm up, loosen up, get their eye in, and they pay the price in the shape of wasted shots.

For me the opportunity to use the practice facilities before the rendez-vous is irresistible. Apart from preparing oneself for that day's game, one can also use all one's clubs, something for which the game itself may not give one an opportunity. For example, sometimes a player goes several weeks without having the misfortune to visit a bunker during a round. When it eventually does happen, he takes hold of his sand wedge, and it feels unfamiliar – which it is. So he shouldn't be surprised if the shot he plays is less than perfect. That being the reality, there is everything to be said for a few minutes on the practice ground, using all types of club, before one does battle with one's friends.

In which connection let me add that some "friends" tend to deride the habit of practising beforehand. Don't fall for this nonsense. They want to stop you preparing properly because they are too idle to do so themselves, but they don't want to suffer for their laziness!

Here's another factor. When I hit a few balls before going out on to the course, it is perfectly normal for me to hit some real stinkers, particularly to begin with. As a result, I discover which particular error I am particularly prone to on that particular day (we all function differently, in my opinion, from day to day). One can perhaps pre-empt the disasters one's imperfect nature may be preparing, by at least being made aware of one's deviant tendencies before the game begins. Forewarned is forearmed.

3: Practice on the course

Never forget that one person, playing alone, 'has no standing', as they say, on a golf course. This means that, when practising on your own, you shouldn't pepper the group ahead with shots, or hold up the group behind. So, as a general rule, try to do your practising on the course at times when it is at its least busy. Another good idea that will prevent you from becoming Public Enemy Number 1 is to repair any damage you might do to greens, fairways and bunkers. I try to do a bit of extra repair work as well – it could be mentioned as a mitigating factor if ever the wrath of the Greens Committee were to be levelled at me.

Practice on the course is extremely valuable. When you are playing a proper game and you do a terrible shot, you can't hold up proceedings while you try to do better. You have to move on, with the taste of disaster hot on your lips. But there is nothing to prevent you slipping out to the same spot on a quiet evening and spending five or ten minutes investigating the whys and wherefores of that particular disaster and working out how to avoid it in future.

There are also plenty of occasions when you want to experiment with different clubs, and different ways of doing things. It is better to do so in quiet isolation where failure costs nothing, rather than risk a volley of abuse from an indignant partner by fluffing an "experimental" shot in the heat of battle at a vital stage in a needle match.

Besides, there is nothing more enjoyable than wandering round an empty golf course on a lovely evening, noticing the changing face of nature and listening to the birds. But don't forget to keep one eye on the group ahead and one on the group behind, if there is one. The secret of practising on the course is to bother nobody. Ideally, one should be invisible. And don't forget to repair the signs of your invisible passing.

I am new to the game of golf, but I have a background that included turf management in another context. I hope that entitles me to express an opinion on the subject. I believe with an absolute fervour that every golfer should always leave the course in better condition than he found it. Not only should he repair the damage he himself inflicts, he should also devote plenty of his idle moments (which are frequent during a round of golf) to repairing the damage done by others.

If every member of a club adopted this attitude, its fairways and greens would be the envy of all the surrounding clubs, and the members themselves would benefit physically, from a lot of extra bending, squatting, prodding, digging and raking.

One caveat: if you spend too much time playing on your own, you are likely to find the presence of your fellow man a distraction, something that interferes with your concentration. So right from the beginning you must seek out opportunities to get out there among the boys (and/or girls) so that you can begin to learn how to block out all their foolish chatter and clatter and movements and coughs and splutters and so on.

"What train?" said Joyce Wethered, and you have to cultivate her sort of insulation against, her sort of withdrawal from, the real world. It's called "being in the bubble" and you have to get inside it every time you play a shot. I will introduce you to Miss Wethered later on.

One other thought about practising on the course. At most clubs, the practice range is fairly flat, so one is almost always hitting shots off level ground. Out on the course there are "up" slopes and "down" slopes, there are left-to-right slopes where the ball is below one's feet and right-to-left slopes where the opposite is the case.

On downland courses, your feet may be on level ground while the ball is on a mini-tumulus a couple of inches higher than your feet, or in a trough a couple of inches lower. Sometimes the ball and your feet are on three different levels. If all your practice has been done on terrain that is uniformly flat, you are going to be disadvantaged when playing on the course – so make sure that plenty of your practice is done there.

Think about potato-peeling. Because of the variations in the shape of the spud, one adjusts one's potato-clutching hand to present the best possible aspect of the vegetable to the blade, and one adjusts one's peeler-clutching hand so that the implement will make its approach at the most effective angle.

In a golf context, the spud (the ground, to you and me) is immoveable, so one has to achieve a perfect contact by one's manipulation of the club, and that involves minute adjustments of the knees, hands, arms and head. There is no way that one can learn that lesson on a flat practice ground.

[After spending time thinking of the best way to convey the idea contained in the last two paragraphs, I spent more time actually writing and re-writing what appears above. A couple of days later the subject occurred to me again as I was gazing at my face's foam-flecked reflection in my shaving mirror. The same principle applies, I surmised, with regard to the ideal angle between razor and skin. I experimented. Believe it or not, within a minute and a half my face (normally like a stubble field) was as smooth as porcelain. This miracle has been repeated, daily, ever since. After forty years of largely wasted effort, I have at last learned to shave. Truly golf is more than just a game!]

Chapter 6

MORE PRACTICE

Like everything else about golf, practice is not a straightforward matter. It is a minefield which demands eternal vigilance on the part of the player, if he or she is to make best use of the possibilities.
Take my experience when I was trying to learn how to develop a long slow backswing, culminating in a pause at the top, followed by a gently accelerating sweep down and through the ball and on to finish with a full follow-through.

I practised it assiduously at home and on the practice ground, and then I went out to play on the course and I was just as assiduous in that stage of the process. And it worked! Provided I resisted the temptation to slash at the ball, I was sending it considerably further and straighter than ever before.

Job done! I congratulated myself, and I was in heaven for a fortnight. Then, mysteriously, the distances I was achieving shrank and my old slice reappeared.

It took about another three weeks before the penny dropped. Happiness over my new swing had turned to anxiety lest I should lose it. Anxiety caused me to shorten the backswing and to restrict the follow-through. So I was back where I had started.

I suppose the moral is that one has to be bold, which can be frightening, and if it works one has to go on being bold, and one must keep pushing oneself until what one is doing becomes comfortable and normal and not at all frightening. And even if one never achieves that comfort zone, one must persist in doing what one knows to be right.

*

The reader could well dismiss my next suggestion as too negative. Feel free to do so, if it doesn't appeal. I find that it helps to have a check-list of the back-slidings to which I am most prone, and to remind myself of them before I go out to do battle.

Currently, my list consists of:
A tendency to grip the club too tight, and to allow tension to affect the moving parts of my body (my arms especially).
A tendency to address the ball with the clubface too "open" (i.e. facing off to the right).
A tendency to "pick up" the club, which is wrong, rather than to "take it back," which is correct.

A tendency to address downhill and uphill shots without recognising the fact that I am not on level ground. Disaster inevitable – think about it. In the case of downhill shots you bury your club in turf three inches behind the ball; uphill, your follow-through hits a brick wall (the planet Earth) after contact with the ball. The remedy is a slight but vital tilt of the stance, and adjustment of the undercarriage. A couple of practice swings will tell you when you are in the right position.

A tendency to lower my head (and/or bend my knees) as I hit the ball, particularly when the ball is below my feet, resulting in the relocation of a considerable chunk of turf, while the ball hardly moves.

Finally, a failure to give short shots (bunker shots especially) a generous backswing and a generous follow-through.

There is nothing to stop one giving oneself a mental nudge in relation to chronic weaknesses as one walks down to the first tee, or as one loosens up before blasting off. Subsequently, as the player approaches his ball, the requirements of the situation should alert him to his most likely mistake, and he can prepare to avoid it. However this last *caveat* should be a momentary thing. When one is about to adopt the position of address, negative thoughts must be banished. Be fearless!

*

Now here's something of vital importance. Several of the great masters of the game have been of the opinion that nothing is more important than the player's grip (the way he holds the club in his hands).

There is also a general consensus (give or take a few minute variations) as to what a correct grip consists of. As a result all club professionals are capable of passing on a sound technique to their pupils.

However, and this is the rub, the correct grip will at first feel uncomfortable to anyone who has not previously used it.

Some of us are so fastidious that we refuse to accept the discomfort, we refuse to put up with the novelty, the strangeness, the awkwardness, that has to be endured for a few weeks, until one gets used to the new arrangement and it becomes the norm and perfectly comfortable.

We resist. We make excuses. "I can't do that," we say, "because my hands are not as other people's hands, nor are my wrists. I used to have piano lessons, you know. I must hold a club thus, and thus and thus, but never ever could I submit to the contortions which this well-meaning but misguided man is trying to impose upon me!"

React in this way and you are guaranteed to be wasting your time on a golf course. Take my word for it. I wasted six years gripping the club "my way" and I was rubbish. Eventually I decided to try to do what I had been told to do six years previously, and the improvement was instant and magical.

Chapter 7

GAMES

From the depths of my ignorance, I suggest that the best sort of game for a novice golfer is called a fourball. Two teams of two players compete against each other, and each of the four players plays his/her own ball. Usually the best player teams up with the worst, against the other two. Whoever wins a hole wins it for his/her side.

Predictably, the better player on each side is expected to outperform his partner, who is the "rabbit". The better player will enjoy this: nobody minds a chance to shine. Consequently the pressure on the "rabbit" is minimal. Most of the time he can hit and miss, potter around, make mistakes, watch and learn, learn, learn.

He has the opportunity to study, and be advised by, higher-class players. That's worth more than diamonds. Almost as valuable, he will learn how to be comfortable in the golfing environment. In addition, he will be hitting plenty of shots, which is a vital ingredient in the learning process.

From time to time he will be called on to play a shot that matters. Occasionally the fate of a hole will depend on his contribution. That will be enough pressure for the time being. As he gets more competent, such occasions will become more frequent, and his ability to handle the pressure will increase accordingly. Golf is a beautiful game. If the novice treats it with respect, it will not go out of its way to be brutal. Well, not often.

One last thing: in your first few months you may be the "rabbit", but you must not for one moment allow yourself to feel inferior. You must take all the time you need to play your shots, and the idea that you must hurry up so as not to keep the others waiting should never enter your head. Hurrying is the mother and father of disaster.

In the early days, preparing to take a shot may feel as though it is time-consuming, but it isn't: the extra time which a novice requires actually only amounts to a few seconds. Besides, if you rush, you will duff the shot, and that will delay proceedings far longer than if you are slow and methodical and produce a better shot.

Having said that, if you have a bad run and have taken seven shots to get into the greenside gorse, while the other three are on the green ready to putt, there is everything to be said for announcing that you are "picking up." Your partner is quite capable of winning the hole without you, so why not? The others get on with it without having to wait for you, while you stand around and reflect on what went wrong, and prepare for the next tee with hope in your heart.

Two more last things, both worth their weight in gold. First, always decorate your golf balls with your private mark.

Words cannot convey the embarrassment which one suffers when one advances on a golf ball and hits it, only to find that it belongs to one of four large angry men approaching from the neighbouring fairway.

Likewise, words cannot convey the indignation when one is on the receiving end of that particular mistake.

There is no end to the misery which stems from the failure to provide one's balls with an identity which is beyond question.

And the opposite is also the case: indisputable ownership equals peace of mind. And if that isn't enough, there is more. Marking balls is fun. One can be as simple or as complicated as one likes. I go for smiling face on one side, glum face on the other. Either way, it's just two dots and a curved line. I walk up to my ball, and it smiles up at me, or it frowns up at me. Often the expression is appropriate to the shot I have just played. Either way, I feel I have a friend. The golf course can be a very lonely place.

Second thing: keep your bag in good order. A golf bag is divided into a number of compartments, usually four, plus a number of pockets, which we will come to later. Each club should belong in one or other of the four compartments. Possibly your arrangement will be: one for the woods; one for putter, sand wedge, and pitching wedge; one for long irons (3,4,5,6); one for short irons (7,8 and 9).

A variety of emotions (rage, elation, disgust, euphoria, bitterness and so on) afflict the golfer during a round. One consequence can be a tendency to hurl clubs into the wrong compartment after use. Result: in a very short time he has no idea what is where, and in a moment of crisis that ignorance will betray him.

He needs a 6 iron, and out of the shambles that is his bag he snatches his 9. He hits a fine shot, but the ball only goes two thirds of the way to the target because he has used the wrong bloody club. Oh dear!

Or maybe he needs his putter in a hurry. He locates it, takes hold and heaves. It refuses to budge. Why? Because for some time he has been shoving every damned club he uses into the same hole and now they've jammed.

Golf is like war: if the basic drills are not working properly, day in and day out, you get flustered – and you get hammered. One of those basic drills requires you to put your clubs back where they belong after use (it's not difficult) and to maintain your bag in perfect order at all times. Do it, or pay the price!

If I were to offer one last thought to the novice golfer of mature years, it would be this: when you go out with your mates to play, or go out on your own to practice, do not be afraid to make mistakes. Trying to develop a new skill is demanding - you must accept that you will make mistakes on the way to working out how to do properly something that is new to you, and difficult.

If you adopt a negative I-must-not-make-a hash-of-this attitude, you will develop a game that is so limited it is hardly worth the effort. Be positive. Make mistakes. Learn from them. Smile. Improve.

*

So, what does the Big Picture amount to so far?
A few minutes of daily practice.
A couple of practice sessions per week, on the practice area or on the course.
A weekly (or maybe twice weekly) fourball, after a warm-up on the practice ground.
All within the framework of your regular tutorials with your teacher.

There you have a six/seven-week launching pad that sets you on your way. And it can be prolonged. If you feel the situation warrants it, you can extend the lessons for several more weeks, or you can arrange a monthly return to the source of all knowledge, so that the teacher has the opportunity to look at you and see if you have fallen into any bad habits, while you pick his brains about things that have cropped up in the intervening weeks.

Golf requires one to think for oneself, but it is a great advantage to have someone to turn to (just a phone call may be enough) when things go wrong. Having glibly written that sentence, let me add a quick *caveat*. The phone can be a deadly weapon. A high-class golf pro may be delighted to meet you for a lesson, out in the open, at a pre-arranged time, for money. But he might find phone calls, especially those that coincide with his dinner, quite intolerable. Check it out. Do nothing that might endanger your relationship with the most important member of your team.

You didn't know you were part of a team, did you? I hope it makes you feel better.

Chapter 8

THE END OF THE BEGINNING

I feel I have introduced you to a structured process which will ensure that your golfing career is launched on a sound basis, with a plan that covers most of the eventualities you are likely to experience in the early stages. I also hope that my contribution will enable you to complete those early stages in two years rather than in ten or fifteen. At our age, this is a consideration of vital importance, is it not?

I am pretty sure that this is the moment for me to retreat into the shadows and leave you to your lessons, your practice and your games. You will be putting in the hours, and out of the hours will come questions and problems and progress and backsliding and more progress. If at times you feel that, for every step forward, you are taking two steps backwards, do not be at all disheartened: this is one of the great golfing experiences and a bond between all players, including the very, very best.

Yes, even the very best sometimes find themselves in the wilderness. Their game deserts them and, however hard they try, they cannot get it back. Sometimes it lasts a month, sometimes a year, sometimes forever. So accept and relish the fact that you are trying to climb a formidable mountain – great fun, but very, very difficult. A basic prerequisite is the ability to take the rough with the rough. Smooth comes later, we hope, and then only in fleeting visits.

Now I suggest you re-read the first six chapters, and go no further until you feel you have got a realistic idea of what you are up against. Until you get to that point, you won't get much value out of my other thoughts and suggestions.

However, before you actually banish this book to the attic, I feel compelled to offer you the first of several items of information that your professional teacher might not consider part of his remit – things that I discovered for myself by trial and error and after quite a lot of pain, which could have been avoided if I had used my brain a bit sooner, or if someone had marked my card.

Let us imagine that you are playing golf in the rain. In the rain you walk on to a wet green and repair your pitchmark with the appropriate tool.

A pitchmark, incidentally, is the indentation which a golf ball produces when it lands heavily on damp turf.

You then mark your ball with the appropriate marker. You pick up the wet ball and you dry it with the appropriate dry rag, which you also use to clean and dry the face of your putter.

When it is your turn to putt, you replace your ball on the green, put away the marker, hit the ball, retrieve it from the cup to a round of applause, move on to the next tee (where you have the honour - the winner of the previous hole tees off first at the next), where you insert the sharp end of your tee-peg (also known as a tee, confusingly) in the turf, balance your ball upon it, and prepare to strike.

So what's the message behind this tale of joy? The message is that you must at all times have all the necessary equipment either on your person or in one of the pockets which decorate your bag, or hanging from various attachments with which most bags are fitted. This is a subject which earlier I promised to deal with in the fullness of time, and that fullness is now. You must also know exactly where every item of your "kit" is to be found. Otherwise the smooth and glorious progress I have described will be anything but smooth and glorious.

You will be sweating with embarrassment because you can't find the pitchmark repairer and as a consequence you are making a mess of the job, using a totally inadequate tee-peg. You will be sweating even more when you can't find a marker for your ball (and you'll be showering the green with handfuls of loose change and fluff while looking for it). An atmosphere of "get a move on" will prevail among your silent companions as you try to dry ball and club on your trousers, and your hurried putt will surely miss the hole.

When you get to the next tee and can't find a tee to place your ball on, your discomfiture will be complete. You will be a broken man and the game will be up, as far as you are concerned, for that day.

Look at the guys around you and you will see how easy it is to keep one's house in order. Simply as a result of basic commonsense and a lot of hours on the golf course, the good players always have all the essential bits of kit, they know exactly where everything is, and finding whatever they need doesn't take any thought at all.

As a result, they have all the time in the world to think about the next shot, and to make the best of it. Unlike the foolish virgin, who cannot escape the nightmare which is the reward for unpreparedness, and who not infrequently ends up seriously disadvantaged.

I have duffed innumerable shots and ruined innumerable rounds by neglecting this very simple aspect of preparation, and my writing will not be in vain if I can save just one novice golfer from a similar fate.

Chapter 9

THREE MONTHS LATER

Three months? Already? It seems like only yesterday.... So, how are things going? Have you thrown in the towel? No? That's good news! What about a teacher - are you in good hands? Which pocket do you keep your pencil in? ... and your marker? What about the pitchmark thingummy? You *are* well organised! Congratulations!

Out of respect for the progress I am confident you have made since last we met, I am going to introduce you to one of the most fundamental and profound elements of the game. Don't hang back – I'm sure you're ready for it.

Bobby Jones is a name that resonates wherever golf is played. He was the Tiger Woods of the nineteen-twenties and thirties. Less well known nowadays is the name of Joyce Wethered (whom I think I mentioned earlier, in rather cryptic terms). At roughly the same period she was the outstanding lady golfer, but she was much more than that. Bobby Jones himself said that she had the best golf swing he had ever seen (man or woman).

He and Joyce once played 18 holes together, at St Andrews, I think, both playing off the men's tees. Jones won by one hole, but at the fifteenth he was two down. When one considers that nowadays the best women seldom (if ever) make the cut in men's events, one gets an indication of the quality of Miss Wethered's play.

Here's a passage from the "History of Golf": "She would come to the first tee, smile charmingly at her opponent and then, almost as though in a trance, become a golfing machine.... Those who played her had the impression that they, the crowd and the state of the game had ceased to exist in her mind and that her entire faculties were being focused on swinging to perfection and holing the ball in the fewest number of strokes... Her seeming remoteness from all the stress and strain that trouble ordinary people bewildered her opponents... Her indifference to what they did became positively nightmarish to them..."

Why do I mention her? As an example of the ultimate in concentration. On one occasion she holed a championship-winning putt just as a train passed on the track alongside the 18th green. Someone asked her if it had distracted her. "What train?" she said.

From us lesser mortals less is expected. However I do think that whenever one walks up to the ball and prepares to play a shot, the rest of the world should simply cease to exist, for the short time that it takes to survey the problem, assess the options, consider the pitfalls, decide on a plan and carry it out.

The fact is that there are quite a number of factors that affect every shot and they all have to be fed into the computer of one's mind. That being the case, the mental machinery (which is limited) must be programmed to ignore everything else. Once the trigger has been pulled, for better or for worse, there will be plenty of time to make conversation, and admire the scenery – before the next shot requires more undivided attention.

Let's go through the basic requirements that every shot demands. As you approach the ball, you are calculating the distance to the hole and the elements – wind in particular. As you reach the ball, the way it is lying is the next factor that matters, and then the condition and shape of the ground on which you will be standing to make the shot. On the basis of all that, you select your club.

In my case a couple of practice swings are meant to help me decide the line along which I intend to propel the ball, the level at which I intend the clubhead to strike the ball and the angle at which I want contact to be made. These thoughts determine my stance. I then do my negative bit: how am I most likely to mess up, and what must I do to prevent that happening. Finally I visualise the right way to play the shot. Then I address the ball and hit it.

If I omit any one of the factors I have listed, I am greatly increasing the chances of ruining the shot. Take my word for it! Let me give you one example: often when I am faced with a short putt which should be easy, I forget to check the level at which the clubhead should travel towards the ball. I omit the practice swing, in my impatience to play the shot. Result: the club scrapes the turf behind the ball, the shot achieves half the power I had intended, the ball fails to reach the hole, and I die a thousand deaths.

I reckon there are ten items that require one's full attention before every shot (as listed above – count them for yourself). It shouldn't be a problem. Most of them can be ticked off in a split second. When one drives a car, flies an aeroplane, does a crossword or fills a supermarket trolley with the goods on a shopping list, one concentrates like mad for hours at a stretch on a wide variety of subjects. Compared with that, thirty or forty seconds of concentration on the same ten items, every few minutes, with plenty of relaxation in between, should be child's play, shouldn't it?

I play regularly with a good golfer, who laughs and chats as much as anyone. But when he walks up to his ball he switches into a different mode, a mode in which there is clearly only one thing on his mind. Off goes the ball, another cracking shot, and he resumes the chat and the laughter.

*

That's enough profundity. Let me offer you something more practical. Dress properly, do not get cold, do not get hot, and treat your bladder with respect.

In 2004, I think, Darren Clarke, the magnificent Northern Irish golfer, decided to lose weight and to "work out". He (or his sponsors) also decided that he needed a new wardrobe. As a result, a slimmer leaner Darren appeared on my TV screen, dressed in very colourful shirts and trousers.

He looked smart, but I got the impression that his trousers were too tight. Maybe his shirts were too tight as well, but that wasn't immediately obvious. Tight clothes worried me. From what little I know about golf, your movement has to be easy and unrestricted, and it cannot be either, if the freedom of your loins and shoulders is restricted by tight trousers and tight shirts (and/or tight sweaters).

In which connection, you will notice when you watch the Major championships on TV that Woods, Els and Mickelson are what might be described as loosely clad. Is that significant? I think so.

Equally important is the question of shoes. They must be well-fitting and comfortable, and they must accommodate thick socks in winter and thin ones in summer, without becoming less well fitting or less comfortable. When you buy shoes, take your time, and think of all those miles that you and they are going to cover together – leave no stone unturned to ensure that your partnership is a friendly one.

On a day which might turn cold, carry sweaters, and put on an extra one (or more) before the cold causes you to play six or seven bad shots. Don't wait for the bad shots to alert you to the drop in temperature.

By the same token, always have gloves in your bag Cold hands cannot hit golf shots.

The reverse is also true. How many times have I found myself sweating, and then playing badly, and finally realised that overheating was partly the cause of the bad shots. As soon as the first hint of sweat beads your brow, remove excess garments and cool down. Simple as that – but it requires eternal vigilance.

As for the bladder, I understand that ladies have a extra problem in this department, which only goes to confirm their superiority. To gentlemen my message is simple. Pee as soon as you feel the first stirrings of the need. Otherwise the need will create tension, and we all know that tension is the enemy of good golf. You will play six bad shots and ruin your round. Then, red faced and disgusted, you will disappear into the bushes, from which you will return relaxed and in perfect condition – but kicking yourself for not having woken up to the situation sooner.

The great Seve Ballesteros was once asked a question. He replied, "Get your breathing right." Unfortunately I cannot remember what the question was. That does not deter me from suggesting that one should never attempt to play a shot when one is gasping, or puffing or panting (or coughing, retching, sneezing). One needs to be calm, stable, balanced. Therefore at all times, while on the golf course, one should bow to the superior judgement of the great Spaniard and get one's breathing right.

Now that I come to think of it, I recall a conversation between Seve and the BBC golf team and he said, "Go to the bathroom." That was in response to another question that has been wiped from the blackboard that once was my memory.

Am I giving you the impression that there is a lot to think about on a golf course? It's the truth. I like to compare every shot to landing a jumbo jet with 340 passengers – neglect just one of the relevant drills and you're in big, big trouble.

What shall we talk about next?

Chapter 10

BOOKS

In the early days of a golfing apprenticeship, it makes sense to confine yourself to your teacher's theories and suggestions.

But as your early days are now behind you, dear reader, you might like to increase your knowledge by reading what some of the finest players and teachers have had to say.

I started this phase in my education by buying the late Harvey Penick's "Little Red Book." Penick was for sixty years the golf coach at the University of Texas. In America, university golf is one of the main channels into the pro game at the highest levels, so he coached a number of top players (Byron Nelson, Tom Kite and Ben Crenshaw to name but three). However he also coached a vast number of the less talented college players, which gave him a profound insight into the problems that face ordinary people (like us). His "Little Red Book" is based on the notes he made throughout his teaching career.

The book is a delight, because each lesson is short and sweet – sometimes only a few lines.

It also jumps from one topic to another in a fairly harum-scarum way, so it is necessary to become familiar with the "Contents" page. This volatility may actually be a good thing, because it doesn't encourage one to go on and on with a reading session (which could cause the mental boiler to overheat and perhaps even explode). So you find the page where he deals with the problem you are struggling with, you read what he has to say, re-read it, try it out, and so on. When exhaustion or revelation occurs, the session ends. There is no undue temptation to turn to the next page because that will be on a completely different subject.

His chapter on bunker play is a classic. In 29 short lines he describes a system that even I can handle, and reduces one of the ordinary golfer's nightmares to the level of "easy-peasy" – well, most of the time. At one stage I photocopied it and sent it to a friend who was having problems in the sand. That good deed was a mistake, and he makes me pay for it with painful regularity.

Some time later I inherited Ben Hogan's "The Modern Fundamentals of Golf." Hogan and Sam Snead were the two stars of the nineteen-forties and fifties, and even today they rank at the top of the heap, in the same class as Arnold Palmer, Jack Nicklaus and now Tiger Woods.

Hogan's co-writer was Herbert Warren Wind, an American sports journalist, and one of the finest writers on the subject of golf. The book is illustrated by the works of someone called Anthony Ravielli. I wish I had a few of his pictures on my walls – they are wonderful works of art.

Hogan presents the essentials of the game with meticulous attention to detail – which was the way he went about playing it, I understand. It is a brilliant book, but harder work than the Penick, because it develops along logical lines, and one is tempted to bite off more than one can chew, and that's where confusion starts. Probably the reader will only start to get the full benefit after he has read it several times. Curiosity satisfied, he will then be more likely to take one chapter at a time, and to stay with a single topic until it has been properly digested.

To me a particularly attractive part of the book is little more than an aside, in which he describes life as a club professional before he went on the pro tour full time. He writes with great delight about the success of one of his pupils, and then, almost wistfully, almost with regret, he speculates about the sort of teacher he might have become if he hadn't been diverted by the prospect of wealth and fame. Truly the game of golf produces more than its share of the most generous people!

My third great tome was written in 1946 or thereabouts by Sam Snead. It mainly consists of sequences of grainy black-and-white film stills of the master playing shots with various clubs, interspersed with his thoughts on how each shot should be played. I had to return the book (now out of print) to its owner, so I spent time and money in the library photocopying practically every page, using A3 paper. Now the Sam Snead Scrolls live on a shelf, rolled up like Magna Carta.

It was widely thought that Snead had the most flexible body of any top-class sportsman, and this attribute (along with his exquisite sense of balance) jumps off the page. The book is another masterpiece of sporting literature.

There is a link between these three books. Snead was Hogan's great rival, and he was also instrumental in Harvey Penick's decision to become a coach. Harvey describes how, as a young man, he toyed with the idea of trying for the pro golf tour. The nub of a section that only covers nine lines runs as follows:

"I walked over to the tee and saw the new kid from West Virginia (Snead) hit his drive. I not only saw it, I heard it. I knew right that moment that my future was not as a tour player."

I also prize, and regularly consult, two books by Tommy Armour, who won Majors between the Great Wars, and then became the most expensive tutor of golfers in the history of the game.

*

The Rules of Golf, a small paperback, is another vital aid. It is given away in the pro's shop of all good golf clubs.

Study it. At first you will be puzzled. Persevere, and in due course you will learn to find your way around. The world is full of idiots who have mastered its secrets, so there is no reason why you and I shouldn't do the same.

I got a copy in my first golfing year, but I left rules and suchlike to my infinitely more knowledgeable companions. However, over a period of time I noticed that there were plenty of occasions when these giants of the fairway were nearly as ignorant as I was regarding the correct procedure in a variety of situations. So, when I got home, I would get out the book and try to work out what we should have done in various situations. If I failed to crack the problem, I would take it to the pro's shop, and if he couldn't give a definitive ruling I would accost the club manager, and so on.

Some people keep a copy of the rules in their golf bag, and there is a lot to be said for so doing. It really does help to be able to refer to the basic rules that cover the most common predicaments that one is likely to encounter.

I would suggest that you start with Rule 28, which explains one's options if one has decided that one's ball is unplayable – a situation quite likely to befall those who are struggling with something new and strange. Reading the rule, and then checking the various references that occur in the explanation of the rule will give you an opportunity to discover how the book works. Each time you go through this process, your knowledge will increase, as will your familiarity with the system.

The novice player's interest in the rules will also become keener when he or she comes up against what may be "suspect behaviour" on the part of fellow players.

Golf is by far the straightest game in the world. The Rule Book gives a clue as to why this is so. Under the heading "The Spirit of the Game" it declares: "Unlike many sports, golf is played, for the most part, without the supervision of a referee or umpire. The game relies on the integrity of the individual to show consideration for other players and to abide by the rules. All players should conduct themselves in a disciplined manner, demonstrating courtesy and sportsmanship at all times, irrespective of how competitive they may be. This is the spirit of the game of golf."

However we live in an imperfect world. I have before me a golf club newsletter of comparatively recent date in which a club captain specifies a series of misdemeanours witnessed on his course. He concludes: "These are not rules being bent, these are rules being broken. If we see rules being broken, we are all under an obligation to point out the error."

This is an obligation which one cannot meet, unless one knows the rules!

Take, for example, the regulation concerning marking one's ball on the putting green, which is dealt with by Rule 20. The Note at the end of the rule states that a ball-marker should be a small coin or other similar object, (placed) immediately behind the ball.

If one finds oneself playing someone who habitually marks the ball with a long tee-peg, laid horizontally on the ground, I defy you to avoid suspecting that somehow or other, in the manipulation involved in marking, lifting and replacing, that ball is going to end up a couple of inches nearer the hole.

That suspicion could well put you off your game, so there is everything to be said for reminding the party concerned about Rule 20 and its very important Note! And of course it's polite to offer the loan of a conventional marker.

The Note also says that, if the ball-marker "interferes with the play, stance or stroke of another player", it should be placed one or more clubhead lengths to one side.

There are those amongst us, however, who misread and misinterpret this sentence. They decide that "clubhead length" means "club length".

"Is my marker in your line? I'll move it."

Whereupon, using his putter, he relocates his marker a full club length (35 inches) to one side, rather than "one or more clubhead lengths". My putter's head measures four and a half inches. So the rule suggests the marker should be a few inches to one side of the ball's original position, but this misinterpretation takes it nearly three feet to one side.

In due course the player reverses the process and restores his ball to somewhere approximating to its original position, and prepares to take his shot.

However, if his trigonometry is not up to scratch, the ball might be anything up to a foot closer to the hole than it should be (or a foot further away, but I suspect that that outcome is comparatively rare.) Why is such a wide margin of error possible? Because, once the first adjustment is made, there is absolutely nothing to show where the ball was originally situated!

The first time you encounter this phenomenon, be thankful if you are not playing for money. The second time, there is no harm in pointing out the difference between a club length and a club*head* length - with a polite allusion to Rule 20.

Rule 13 is also full of exciting, and maybe even inflammatory, potential – but I leave you to research that one on your own.

Chapter 11

SOMETHING DIFFERENT

As a rule I do not pontificate on matters which directly involve the actual playing of the game of golf, because of my ignorance.

However, there are occasions when I cannot resist the temptation to overreach myself – for the benefit of the reader, I hasten to add. This is one of them. Let us think for a moment about the swing that launches the ball in the direction of the hole, when one is trying to advance it quite a long way.

The number one significant factor is the length of the swing. Within reason and within the limitations of one's physical condition, the further back you take your backswing and the further up-and-over you carry your follow-through after hitting the ball, the greater the club-head-speed that will have been built up, effortlessly, and the further the ball will travel.

Who is this idiot, you must be asking yourself, who denies that he pontificates and immediately starts doing just that?

Listen to this: "The one quality a golf swing must have is smoothness. The acceleration from the top must be gradual. ...the motion must be unhurried and free from any sudden or jerky movements.... The clubhead must have plenty of time to gather speed before it reaches the ball. It is apparent that the longer the arc through which the club travels, the less need there will be for any abnormal expenditure of energy at any one particular instant...."

I didn't write that. Bobby Jones did. As you know, he was one of the greatest golfers ever, and a man of considerable intellectual powers as well. If he said something, it usually made sense. I forgot to mention the sixth golfing "bible" in my library. "Bobby Jones on Golf" is based on newspaper articles he wrote between 1927 and 1935. It was published as a book in 1966, and is still in print because it is superb.

Impressed? May I continue describing the swing? Thank you.

You stand there, holding a club. A light grip with your hands and not an iota of tension in any part of your body. Turning your shoulders and hips, you take the club ever so slowly back and up as far as is comfortable. And as you do so you cock your wrists, comfortably. If there is no tension in your trunk and limbs, the shaft will end up somewhere behind your head.

An infinitesimal pause and the downswing begins and gathers pace and eventually the wrists uncock (which adds to the speed of the clubhead) and the clubhead sails through the ball and continues on its way, in the direction of the target, and then up and over as it completes the follow-through, until the shaft is once again behind your head.

I cannot emphasise too strongly that at no stage in this process are you to allow tension, effort or strain to enter the proceedings.

Most adult novice golfers (like me) die of fright at the very idea of what I have just described. "If the club is behind my right ear one moment," they complain, "and behind my left ear a moment later, how can I possibly make contact with a small white ball at my feet?"

Take a hike into your back garden. Arm yourself with a club that you are reasonably comfortable using. Say a fond farewell to the dandelions and begin to behead them.

Nothing frantic, nothing energetic. Loose grip, loose muscles, slow movement, good balance, no effort, and as long an arc as is comfortable.

You'll miss a few at first. It may take a day or two before you start to get your eye in. But very soon you will find that you cannot miss. This proves that you can comfortably wind a club round the back of your neck twice in fairly quick succession, and smack a dandelion with unwavering precision in between.

The alternative to the long swing is the short one. What have I got to say about that? Nothing. What did Bobby Jones have to say about it?

"The average golfer, partly because he does not trust himself, almost always favours a short hacking stroke. Quickly back and quickly down, employing a sudden acceleration almost amounting to a jerk. There is scarcely any chance of obtaining power or accuracy."

Think "Long, Slow and Easy." After a period of trial and error, and a certain amount of disappointment, that little white ball will pleasantly surprise you by how far it goes, and how straight it goes.

The doom merchants will cast doubt on the wisdom of going for "L, S and E". They will suggest that the suppleness of youth is essential if one is to pivot the trunk and stretch the arms sufficient unto the requirements of the enterprise.

It's rubbish born of ignorance, or possibly of fear and jealousy. They don't dare to enter unknown terrotory, and they would prefer you to be as negative as they are.

This is a matter in which it is possible to compromise. There may be periods when you cannot bring yourself to use a long swing. Fair enough. The more you jab and stab, the sooner you will realise how limiting and how unsatisfactory it is. Just keep going back to the long swing from time to time, keep practising it until it clicks into place. Keep practising it until you can treat the little white ball as if it was a dandelion. You will never regret it.

While on the subject, here's an aside which may be of some value. I find that music helps me to achieve rhythm in my shots and prevents me from hurrying them. For long shots (with woods or irons), as I prepare to hit I imagine I can hear Buddy Holly singing "Heartbeat".

"Heartbeat / why do you miss / when / my baby kisses me?"

"Heartbeat" is the waggle at address, if you are a waggler. If you aren't, it's the quiet moment you spend at address before the machinery starts to move.

"Why do you miss" is the backswing.

"When" is the pause as backswing ends and the return journey is about to begin.

"My baby kisses me" is the club accelerating through the ball and into the follow-through.

Contact between clubhead and ball happens on the "kiss" of "kisses" – rather appropriate, don't you think?

Buddy Holly is not mandatory. Go for whatever music suits the movement, makes you comfortable and does you good. Anything that stops you rushing your shots is worth its weight in gold. For example, there is magic in the first few notes of the second movement of Mozart's Piano Concerto No. 20 in D minor.

Chapter 12

A MIXED BAG

Time has passed, much has happened, and I am confident that, in terms of golf, you are in good shape. You may see things differently: you may be in despair, the result of a series of disappointments. That doesn't matter. You have a structure to your arrangements, and in time that structure will surely sustain you. However dark the clouds "that lour upon your house" (W. Shakespeare, Richard III, more or less), there is light at the end of your golfing tunnel.

Clubs, Lessons, Clubs, Practice 1, Practice 2, Fourballs, Books - and the guiding hand of a Master Professional will see you through. Work hard and fear naught.

My next offering is in the form of a series of mini essays. I will convey to you, in thin slices, a fund of information which I acquired over ten years and at the cost of much sweat, toil and tears. It will become yours in a matter of minutes and at no cost at all either in sweat, toil and tears or in money (this book was very, very cheap, and may already be worth more than it cost.)

I look back at those fairly painful years, and I say to myself, "If, when I started, someone had been kind enough to mark my card as regards these golden nuggets of vital information, I could have got where I am today in two years, instead of in ten, and would have escaped much of the trauma which has marred my progress and seriously reduced my potential! In addition, I would perhaps have avoided much of the disdain, contempt and derision which has been launched in my direction by my fellow golfers for as long as I can remember."

But I'm not bitter.

*

Let's start with something that I was reminded of this morning. A hooked drive ended in semi-rough under some trees. On arrival at the crime scene, I took out my five wood and waved it, to see if my swing was impeded by overhanging branches. There was not even the whisper of a caress between clubhead and greenery.

So I addressed the ball, took the club back.... And staggered sideways as the shaft was rocked in three directions at once, like the mast of a ship in a tempest, by the foliage behind my right shoulder.

70

The lesson? When you do your speculative "Am I clear?" practice swing, make it as full and as fierce as your "real" swing is going to be. And repeat the investigative gyration several times. I suspect that, because we don't want to find that we are in trouble, we subconsciously cramp our practice swing. Let's not do that. It is costly. Let us look the truth straight in the face. It gives one the chance to work out a strategy for avoiding disaster.

*

My next essay needs an introduction, as follows: "To play golf, you have to have a good temperament. If nothing upsets you, as appears to be the case with Ernie Els, you have a good chance of playing well. If lots of things upset you, like Colin Montgomerie, you are much more likely to fall in a heap." End of introduction.

The first time I entered a competition, I was beaten, 7 down with 6 to play (thrashed), by a man with long hair. When I asked around afterwards, I was given the impression that he was nothing out of the ordinary. So why had he thrashed me?

On the first tee he introduced himself, banged his drive down the middle, and as soon as my ball was airborne he marched off the tee at s hundred miles an hour. Impressed by the pace of competitive play - this was my first taste, remember - I marched in pursuit.

Somehow his speed between shots soon began to affect not only my speed between shots, but also the speed with which I played the shots themselves. No wonder I was thrashed.

The moral? Go your own pace. If he rushes, you amble. If he doesn't waste any time over his shots, that is no reason for you to follow suit. If the difference between you is going to cause a disadvantage to either party, let it be to him and not to you! I would go so far as to suggest that, the faster the opponent plays and walks, the slower you should play and walk. Stick it to him, in fact!

On reflection, the above is a fairly adequate comment on the pace of play, but it only scratches the surface of the subject of good temperament. Imperturbability is the quality one needs to cultivate. This means that whatever happens (fights, gunfire, chronic delays, blatant cheating, stray dogs running off with balls, constant chatter, World War 3), one maintains that calm, relaxed concentration which is essential if one is to hit nothing but nice shots. Some people are born with good temperament. The rest of us have to work at it.

*

A word on mistakes. You make a mistake and allow it to fester in your mind. Bloody hell, you mutter again and again, how could I have been so stupid? Immediately one mistake becomes four, because festering takes up brain space, at the expense of one or more of the important things you need to be thinking about in connection with your next three shots.

If you don't know why you made the original error, there is no point dwelling on it. Sort it out tomorrow, in practice. If you do know the reason, there is even less point in dwelling on it. The requirements of the rest of the round mean you cannot afford to give brain space to beating yourself up or to *post mortems*.

*

"He's all right until he gets a card in his hand" is a well-known saying in golfing circles. Quite a lot of players don't bother to keep a strict record of scores on a card in their "social" games, or when playing Matchplay (when holes won and lost decide the issue, and the number of shots taken for the whole round doesn't matter).

As a result, the card becomes a signal that this is an important round, for one reason or another (usually a Medal round [monthly competition], or an attempt to reduce one's handicap, or a game where money is at stake).

For a sizeable number of people this signal activates a self-destruct button. Show them a card and they become shadows of their usual golfing selves. It's a fact.

The answer? As often as possible carry a card. As often as possible keep a score. Do not let the sight of a card and a pencil frighten you. Let familiarity breed indifference.

*

Same thing, different aspect. Most Medal rounds and other competitions are played off the "White" tees (which means you drive from the white markers at each hole). The White markers are usually ten or fifteen yards behind the Yellow markers which are used in non-competition play. So each hole is a few yards longer than you are used to.

Some players freeze at the very mention of "White Tees". This is a pity because the extra yardage is seldom of any real significance. It's a psychological thing.

The answer? Use the White tees regularly. Once again, let familiarity breed indifference. At the club to which I belong, nowadays one is free to tee off from the white markers, even when not in a competition - so I do. Regularly. It is amazing how quickly one becomes indifferent to the extra few yards.

In previous years, the White tees were for competitions only, and I believe that this is the rule at many clubs. In those days, if I found myself alone, with no trace of a Committee member or greenkeeper in sight, I would ignore the rule, and it did me good. As I have always been in the habit of visiting the course early and late, and during bad weather, I had plentiful opportunities to expose my fragile psyche to the extra demand that those little white markers imposed. Problem solved.

*

Some players get to the halfway point in a round in very good shape: no mistakes and a low score. Whereupon into their minds slides the poisonous reptile known as Expectation. My goodness, says the player, this could be my best round ever. <u>If I keep it up</u>, I am going to break 100 (or 90, or 80)!! The immediate consequence is a tensing up of all the moving parts, both mental and physical – with disastrous results.

The cure is simple, but quite difficult to apply, so work at it. No round exists until it is finished, in the same way that no flight across the Atlantic is finished until the pilot and passengers feel terra firma under their feet. It's no use them congratulating themselves on a safe journey while 30,000 feet up with Ireland under the port wing. So it is with golf. The player must accept, without reservation, the fact that the work of art he is creating is in constant danger of total destruction until it is completed and the varnish has dried.

The player's attention belongs to the next shot for as long as there is a next shot. Expectation interferes with the job in hand. Every time you do a good shot, take time to pat yourself on the back – then go back to war, and stay on a war footing until the last shot has been fired!

*

By the same token, there is a tendency to play three good shots in succession, and then to tell yourself that you've cracked it! You will immediately drop your guard and you will immediately be punished. Until the round is over, you are in danger. Drop your guard and you are a dead man. Every shot requires 100% concentration. There is no value in a good shot. There is only value in a good round and there is no such thing as a good round until it is over.

*

One more point, and then we definitely leave the asylum. You are happy as Larry, playing well, nice weather, good company. Suddenly your group notices that the group ahead are waving. What does it mean? It means that they have lost a ball and are intent on finding it. So they want you to "play through", so that you will not be unduly delayed.

It is normal practice, but the novice can find it traumatic. The tendency is to hurry, and to be aware of four players, waiting on the edge of the fairway, watching every move you make – possibly your first experience of an audience, in a golfing context.

The remedy? Do not hurry. Instead of panicking at the prospect of hitting one of these polite people with a wayward shot, concentrate on your normal routine, and your chances of murdering somebody will become negligible. After all, they are watching every move you make, so they have a sporting chance of dodging small white flying projectiles. Stay calm. They have invited you to play through, not to rush through.

Imperturbability – it cannot be repeated too often - is a very valuable quality, well worth cultivating.

"Don't upset yourself," says the guest to the host who has come down to breakfast to find that the speaker has filled in his crossword puzzle. The theory is that any cardiac acceleration could be fatal. The same applies on the golf course. Make it a golden rule never ever to become disconcerted.

Chapter 13

"WEATHER 'TIS NOBLER IN THE MIND TO SUFFER..." (With apologies to Wm Shakespeare)

Learning how to play when the wind is blowing is a fascinating exercise, and handling the tempest competently is immensely satisfying. That is the inspirational and glorious reason for learning to play in windy weather. The sordid, practical and exploitative reason is to be found in the fact that most golfers hate the wind, many of them think it is unfair, quite a few won't play when there is more than a whisper of moving air, and the majority of those who will are beaten before they start, such is the depression that wind produces – so they are sitting ducks for anyone who comes to the party properly prepared and with an appetite for the challenge.

I truly relish playing in windy conditions and practising in them, and it is not just because I have the course largely to myself, although that is a considerable plus. It is simply great fun adjusting one's aim to take account of the direction in which it is blowing, trying to keep the ball low when facing the storm, and popping it up high when it is giving one a helping hand.

In the latter case in particular, one has an extra puzzle to make sense of: wind-power means adjusting the power of one's shots, and the clubs one uses. It makes one think – and that makes one a better person.

I suppose that to a certain extent wind for the golfer is like wind for the sailor: if you know what you are doing you get a great kick out of managing this unruly element in a constructive fashion.

As one duffer to another, my only bits of advice to you are these: first, take time on the tee to stabilise your position, so as not to be blown off balance when you swing; second, when hitting into wind, do not expect to hit the ball as far as you would on a still day. And do not try to make up the deficit by increased effort. Just use a "bigger" club. If the distance calls for a 6 iron, let the wind persuade you to use a 4. Or just accept that you may need an extra shot per hole into the wind, and just possibly one less shot with the wind helping. All you should concentrate on is good contact between bat and ball.

Actually I have one other bit of advice. When the wind is knocking you backwards, pretend it's helping you. Say to yourself, "So nice to have a following wind! I don't need to slog." Then don't slog, and you will probably be pleasantly surprised.

*

What about cold weather? Simple – it is impossible to play golf if you are cold, particularly if you have cold hands.

I swear by Long Johns. With good thick socks below and an extra pair of underpants clinging to the lower abdomen, they create warmth that spreads all over the body. As a result, one doesn't have to overload the upper body and arms, so one retains full freedom of those vital assets. Above the waist, I usually just wear a short-sleeved thermal vest, a thick shirt, one sweater, a short scarf and a quilted waistcoat (which has very handy pockets). Add a woolly hat and loose gloves that can be put on and taken off in an instant, and the cold ceases to be a factor. Or rather, the cold starts to be an asset, because it penalises those who haven't prepared for it – and hopefully your opponents will be in that category!

Warm headgear is important. Skiers, mountaineers and explorers are unanimous that in cold weather one loses 25% of one's body heat through one's head, if left uncovered. Be warmed... I mean warned.

As with wind, so with cold: those who have come to terms with the rougher edges of the weather find they have the course almost entirely to themselves whenever the mercury drops, which is a bonus.

*

What about rain? You need a good mindset. Perhaps because I wear glasses, I decided at an early stage in my golfing life that I couldn't play in rain. After five years, during which I had improved my headgear so that hardly a drop of water got onto my glasses, I realised that the formula "rain equals loss of form because of blurred lenses" didn't hold water (if you'll pardon the play on words).

My bad play was nothing to do with eyesight, nor was it anything to do with rain. I had decided that I was at a disadvantage in the wet, and had reacted by gripping the club too tight. Tension soon spread to the rest of the body, and disaster became inevitable.

As soon as I faced the fact that I wasn't disadvantaged, I relaxed. As soon as I relaxed, my normal performance (not great, but adequate) resurfaced. Anyone can play reasonably well in normal sort of rain, provided they believe they can.

On a practical level, wet conditions call for good waterproof shoes and a suit of efficient waterproofs (jacket and trousers). Also a cover over the top of one's bag (I rather think I want to try a transparent one, so that I can locate the club I am after before I have to expose the contents of the bag to the elements), and several little towels to dry hands, balls, grips and clubfaces.

Incidentally, if you are trying to hit out of wet rough (or semi-rough), close the face of the club a tad. This week, in the wet, in the semi-rough, I took the view that the important thing was to get the ball up in the air, so I opened the face. Three times running the ball sped off to the right (hard right) without leaving the ground. I was circling the green like a demented sheepdog. It was only then that my friendly mentor (and opponent) shouted across, "In the wet, close the face!"

"Now he tells me," I muttered bitterly. There is nothing like wet semi-rough and bitterness for etching a lesson permanently on one's psyche.

*

"Rage, rage against the dying of the light," advised Dylan Thomas. I wouldn't go quite that far, but this is an aspect of the natural world that the golfer would be unwise to ignore.

In winter there are days that are gloomy from dawn to dusk, in summer there are games that last till well after the first stars have appeared.

The prudent golfer should carry a sensitive light meter in his head. As the shadows deepen, he should pay more and more attention to the simple tasks of looking at the ball, inspecting the lie of the land, and checking the position of the club face at address.

At the other extreme is blinding sunshine, which I find extremely difficult. However, it is not all bad. As long as you are looking at the ball at address, sunshine cannot hurt your shot. The brighter the sun, the more reason to concentrate on the ball during the stroke, and to keep looking down until the shot is well and truly finished. Someone else can be responsible for noting where the projectile returns to earth.

Chapter 14

WEIGHT FOR IT
BEWARE THE WOUNDED GOLFER
CREAM CRACKERS

As you know, it is not my intention to teach you how to play golf: that I leave to the experts whom you have chosen to guide you. So far, my only intervention in that area has been to suggest that you give serious consideration to the advantages of a long, slow swing. I cited Bobby Jones as the authority whose opinion on the subject I was simply passing on.

It is now my intention to encourage you to go further along that particular road by recommending "the heavy club." In this case the authority whom I am citing is the late Harvey Penick, a teacher to whom I introduced you in the section on books. He wrote: "Every golfer, from the young adult through Seasoned Citizens, should have a heavy practice club that weights at least 22 ounces.....

"It hardly needs to be said," he continued, "that a heavy club is no good for children....(But) swinging a weighted club, with your regular grip and stance, is the best exercise I know to build golf muscles... Every time you swing that weighted club, slow or moderately fast, aim the clubhead at a fixed spot. Learn a good habit while you are building golf muscles."

All I can add is an account of what happened to me when I followed his advice. I made my own "heavy" club by locking a chunky steel padlock round the bottom of the shaft of a hideous driver that I had given up using. I then taped the padlock to the clubhead so that it couldn't move.

On reflection, it occurs to me that I didn't consult the experts as to the design of this weapon and the positioning of the additional weight. No harm came of it, but the reader would be well advised to adopt a more cautious approach than I did. Take advice.

In the garden I would address a dandelion. I will re-phrase that, before the men in white coats take me away. I would adopt the "address position" in relation to a dandelion.

Turning my shoulders and pivoting at the waist, I would then take the club slowly back and up and round, pause at the top, then reverse the turn, feel the club gather speed as gravity and my gentle encouragement affected it, catch the yellow flower full in the face and send it flying in the right direction (hopefully), and then allow the weight of the clubhead to pull me into the proper follow-through position.

What did it do for me?

Let's start at the end of the story. Previously, my standard reaction to a hefty swipe was one quick pace backwards to prevent myself from overbalancing. Why I was pouring energy in that direction was (and still is) a mystery. It was only with the help of the heavy club that I started to do the follow-through easily, naturally, and in the direction of the target. It improved my accuracy, added considerably to the length of my shots, and stopped me looking drunk and disorderly whenever I tried to hit the ball a long way.

When first I handled the heavy club, I stiffened the sinews in anticipation of a heavy load. This tended to make all the moving parts stiffen up, which made turning and lifting rather an ordeal.

So I tried what Florida guru David Leadbetter calls "soft arms" – relaxed sinews, tendons, muscles – and lifted the club like that. It went back, round and up just as easily as before, and the other moving parts involved in the process seemed to enjoy it rather more than the earlier attempts.

Because the club is heavy, it is natural to take it back slowly. This provided an insight into just how slowly it is possible to swing a club. Bobby Jones said, "Nobody ever swung a golf club too slowly," which is a saying that has a certain element of the occult about it. But the longer one plays the game the more one understands what he meant. For the moment let us just say that "long and slow" (especially for the backswing) is desirable, and a heavy club helps one achieve it.

So, having completed the movement a number of times with the heavy club, one discards it and picks up one's normal driver or long wood, and one mimics what one has just done, and at the same speed and to the same rhythm (and to the same inner music, perhaps).

The club seems as light as a feather, raising it requires no effort, no tension, no strain, one has all the time in the world to fit in the minor adjustments which the swing demands from knees, hips, back and shoulders. The return journey is equally facile and smooth, and the inevitability of a full follow-through is like a delightful invitation to the dance. Am I beginning to talk rubbish?

Finally a word of warning: don't try to hit hard with your heavy club. It makes you tense up and heave. I made this mistake once only: one violent and misguided session in the garden, and the next day on the course I couldn't hit the ball at all. I was heaving like a very inebriated sailor. I thought it was the end of the world.

That evening I put two and two together and recognised the error of my ways. I went out into the garden and just swung, long and easy, with the heavy club – aiming "through" a blade of grass or whatever. Just feeling the easy, unhurried rhythm: all the way back and all the way through. Then I picked up a driver and hit a few practice balls, and normal service was restored: long, slow, light as a feather, effortless, full follow-through. What a relief.

*

When one is of a certain age, there are days when one feels "out of sorts" (for want of a better description). Dull, flat, weak. The good news is that there is no reason to write off such days. Resist the temptation to pull the blankets over the head and turn towards the wall. The golf course is still the place for you.

There are several reasons why one plays surprisingly good golf on bad days. The first is this: "out of sorts" people become fearless. Instead of succumbing to a variety of apprehensions before each shot (those trees, that gorse, two bunkers and a water hazard – Oh my God!), one is so deflated that one couldn't give a toss for any of them. One picks one's target and swings. In a phrase, one ignores the negatives – which is not a guarantee of a good result, but the next best thing.

In addition, the worn-out, broken-down sportsman is more inclined to apply himself drearily but doggedly to the routine that relates to each shot. Unlike days when he is full of the joys of spring, he has no wish to indulge in careless rapture. Instead, he dourly, grimly and thoroughly calculates and adjusts and visualises and rehearses and checks and double-checks. This approach, too, is no guarantee of success, but it helps.

There is another take on the subject which may, or may not, be relevant. Most amateur golfers fail to reach the green with their third shot at a par five (for example), not because they haven't the power, but because they haven't taken enough club. It's a macho thing of pandemic proportions which has existed since golf began.

For example: "140 yards – I can get there with my six-iron – but my bull-necked opponent goes for it with his seven, so I will too!" As stupid as that!

Well, when you're feeling hung-over or otherwise indisposed, the testosterone is abnormally quiet and gives the brain a chance. You use your six – and win the hole. The principle applies to a multitude of club selection situations.

Under the weather? Get out there and play! If the worst comes to the worst and nothing goes right, the very fact that our invalid has managed eighteen holes without falling by the wayside is quite enough to put a spring in his step. It is cheering to find out that one may be out of sorts, but one isn't at death's door.

*

Let me stray a little further down the lane marked "Psychology". You will meet plenty of male players who are inordinately proud of the distance they can hit the ball. Describing their endeavours off the tee, they will use expressions like "I really creamed it."

Encourage them. The more often they cream it, the more often will the prodigious distance they achieve be in quite the wrong direction.

*

That reminds me of visualisation, a process widely recommended by a number of reputable golf coaches. When you prepare to hit a shot, they advise, you should pause and visualise the swing, the contact, the flight of the ball, the landing, the forward scuttle and the return to inertia.

A word of warning, ladies and gentlemen. Do not visualise anything that is far beyond your capabilities. The result will be a mighty heave and a feeling of nausea as the ball squirts out sideways without leaving the ground.

You must pick a target area that you know is within your range. The moment you do so, you will relax. The moment you relax, your potential increases, and you may well give yourself a nice surprise – again, and again, and again!

*

A thought occurs to me - possibly triggered by the mention of the "heavy club." When one reaches a certain age, one's physical rate of recovery after exercise slows down. So, if you give yourself a hard time on a Tuesday, don't expect to be all the better for it by Wednesday morning, as would have been the case when you were twenty. It might take till Friday before you start bucking and squealing. Nothing to worry about – go with the flow.

Chapter 15

WHAT ELSE IS NEW?

I am the most obsessive person I know. If I have something bothering me, I cannot read a book, or watch television, or sleep, without my mind bouncing back to whatever it is at every opportunity – which is a bore.

The one thing that can spirit me away from my current obsession is the golf course. As soon as I can feel turf underfoot and see the elegant patterns of a new-mown fairway, I am released from the slings and arrows. My mind only has eyes for the next shot, the strength of the wind, the quality of the sand, the unfathomable mysteries of camber and borrow, not forgetting the changing tints of autumn leaves and the magic of a hovering kestrel – plus a few more immediate phenomena, like the slow play of the group ahead, or the irritating habit of one of my opponents (he coughs every time I putt. Is this coincident or is the bastard up to something?)

When the game is over and I come back down to earth, I am rested, relaxed, fresh, ready to wrestle with my obsession and to face anything that malicious fate may throw at me. One cannot put a price on a tonic of such beneficial potency.

Talking of gentleman who cough, let us suppose you are thinking of rowing across the Atlantic with a new friend. I suggest you spend a few hours playing golf with him (or her) before you commit yourself. There is no better way of establishing compatibility, or the opposite, than by spending time together on fairways, in bunkers, around greens, or deep in the rough; in fair weather and foul; for fun, or for money.

And you certainly should apply the golf test before going into business with anybody. Watching a comparative stranger as he faces the ordeal of extricating himself from deep, juicy rough, perhaps unconscious of the fact that he is being watched, can convey a whole library of valuable information.

*

But that's enough about them. The green, green grass of golf will also tell you more about yourself than you might expect. There will be surprises, some nice, most not so nice.

Your ability to take the rough as well as the smooth in your stride will be subject to a severe examination every time the golfing gods decide to punish you for no apparent reason. Do not worry. If you can take it, it will do you good. If you can't – let the tantrum which explodes be the first step in a programme of character-rebuilding. Golf is always trying to make you a better person. Hang in there, and you will become less and less vile the longer your golfing life continues. When it is over, you will have stockpiled sufficient virtue to see you through to the end – and hopefully beyond.

*

Change of subject. You find yourself on the green, your ball three feet from the hole. The green slopes from left to right. In these circumstances you have two options: you can aim towards the left edge of the hole and stroke the ball softly, relying on the slope to turn it into the hole; or you can aim for the middle of the hole and give it a sharp rap – speed will neutralise the influence of the slope. But you can't combine the two methods. The other day I tried to. I aimed for the left edge and rapped it sharply – the ball sailed past the hole and off the green altogether. It was just a reminder that at a certain age the need to guard against intermittent lunacy increases.

The good news in that regard is this: a scientist in Sweden has recently published research findings which suggest that fifty-somethings (and upwards) who take up extra exercise on a regular basis slow down the advance of senility. I am a living breathing example of what he is talking about, and golf is my chosen weapon in the struggle for mental and physical survival. I cannot recommend it too strongly. I also attack a daily crossword.

*

I rather like to play for small sums of money. For example, a fourball where each player puts a pound in the kitty. It's something to do with incentive. If one is trying to improve one's game, winning or losing is a rough indicator of one's progress, and a small reward for doing well is encouraging, gives one a bit of a glow, recharges the batteries, justifies the time spent practising, and makes one concentrate just that little bit harder on the way round. And paying out when you lose cannot help but concentrate the mind.

*

On balance (says he, changing the subject yet again) I would advise the average veteran newcomer to the game of golf to avoid becoming the life and soul of the party. Even if you are a raconteur of genius, my suggestion is that you leave this talent in the clubhouse. By all means be polite, correct, courteous, friendly. But by the time you reach the first tee let it be clear that your mind is on the job in hand.

Otherwise you may be tempted to launch into a humorous anecdote, which will act as a signal to your companions that you are in the mood for frivolity and will surely enjoy whatever they may have to offer in that department.

Before you know it, the sound of cheerful laughter will be echoing across the greensward and you will be marooned in double-bogey-land because your concentration will be non-existent. Golf requires single-mindedness.

"Stiffen the sinews, summon up the blood, disguise fair nature with hard-favoured rage. Then lend the eye the terrible aspect. Let it prise through the portal of the brow as doth the brass cannon o'erhang and jutty its confounded base, swilled in the wild and wasteful ocean."

Shakespeare tends to over-egg the pudding. All I would suggest is that you keep an eye on your golfing companions. Over a period of time I suspect you will find that it is the quiet ones, those who seem somehow a trifle withdrawn, a trifle preoccupied, that win the prizes.

Chapter 16

MORE STRENGTH TO YOUR ELBOW

When I started playing golf, in my late fifties, I used to carry my clubs. After a time I decided that this was too much like hard work. In addition I was told (at one time people talked of little else) that if I used the golfbag's basic bog-standard sling for carrying, and if I habitually used one shoulder rather than changing from one to the other at regular intervals, I would in time develop a one-sided posture. Advancing years should not be given any encouragement in that direction.

I tried using one of those harnesses that are designed to spread the load across both shoulders. It helped. Even so – hard work.

For a long while I used an ordinary trolley (the sort that relies on its owner for propulsion), but I hated it. In the game of golf one expects one's arms to be relaxed, flexible and full of energy whenever required. In that context, I found the stretch and strain by a loaded trolley very uncomfortable. Worse than uncomfortable: I thought the trolley was hindering my best efforts to improve my game.

So carrying and dragging were unsatisfactory. Needless to say, it hadn't escaped my notice, when watching television, that professional golfers neither carry nor drag. Did they know something that I was beginning to suspect?

That was my situation when I played a few games with an ex-sportsman (fairly recently retired), who took his golf just as seriously as he had his earlier sporting activities. Exceptionally intelligent and a perfectionist, he applied himself wholeheartedly, and his handicap at the time was heading towards single figures.

A year or so later the word reached me that he had resorted to a battery-powered trolley. According to the story, this was because he was suffering from the after-effects of an old sporting injury.

I decided that the old injury was a fairy tale. Not that I had any evidence. I just have a suspicious nature and a fertile imagination. According to my theory, this very intelligent chap had come to the same conclusion that I had: that carrying or dragging one's clubs adversely affects one's game. So he had motorised himself.

Why the fairy tale? This, I decided, had been for two reasons. First, so as to prevent his sporting mates and ex-colleagues from pointing the finger of scorn (sportsmen tend to resist any suggestion of human frailty or advancing years), and, second, in order to conceal the advantages of motorisation from people whom he might well be in the habit of playing for significant sums of money. I've got a sick mind, haven't I?

A couple of years later, one of my golfing companions died, and on his deathbed he left his electric trolley to a long-time neighbour and friend.

During the following year the friend (who had been seriously lame for many decades) grew somewhat lamer, and then lamer still, until eventually he accepted the need for a buggy (a motorised conveyance for player as well as clubs) whenever he played.

One day, as we were leaving the course, he turned to me and said, "Would you like a motorised trolley?"

"More than anything else in the world," I replied, exaggerating only a tiny bit.

It transpired that he had never used his legacy, and saw no prospect of using it in the future.

"It's in my shed," he said, "plus battery and charger. Pick it up any time."

Three days' later was any time enough for me, and my first day as the proud owner of this Rolls Royce among trolleys confirmed all my theories. One's arms stay fresh as a daisy. One's clubs are always available as though being offered by the most obliging of caddies, but at no cost.

The various contents of the various pockets of one's bag are also so much more readily available than had previously been the case. There is no doubt in my mind that a motorised trolley is a wonderful investment for any middle-aged newcomer to golf, and as far as I know they last forever, which is a bonus.

I have a friend who plays off a handicap of 15 (fairly competent) and he, being of the same opinion as myself, advised a friend of his, a 3-handicapper (seriously good) to invest in a motorised trolley. The latter in due course reported that this accessory had improved his average performance by two shots per round. 3-handicappers compete very near the top level of the game, where an improvement of 2 shots a round is significant, and a 3-handicapper is quite likely to know what he is talking about when he attributes this improvement to a bit of machinery.

Think about it, O reader, and bear in mind that two shots for a 3-handicapper could convert into significantly more for players at a lower level – all else being equal.

I have to confess, however, that it hasn't worked the oracle for me – yet. I was on a 20 handicap when I got my trolley, and that is where I remain. But the new-found bounce in my step is unmistakable.

Although I have only had this triumph of engineering a little more than a year, I am in a position to pass on a few tips. My machine doesn't seem to have a handbrake. It can run away if left on a slope, even if the motor is switched off. So one must remember to turn it sideways.

More important, going up steep slopes it can fall over backwards (the weight of the clubs is just enough to unbalance it), so it pays to keep a hand on or behind the joystick, just in case. When it does tip up and lie on its back with its wheels rotating madly in the air, stay calm. Go straight for the "on/off" switch and put it out of its misery. Any other move will only compound the disaster. It took me a while to learn that.

I might add that it takes a little time to achieve harmony between man and machine as regards the pace of one's wanderings. The secret is to let the machine dictate the terms. One has to acquaint oneself with its little ways, which are based on certain fundamental facts of life. For example, it will chug steadily up hills at a certain throttle setting, but once it reaches level ground at the top that setting will cause it to accelerate alarmingly. A downturn in the terrain will have a similar effect. So one is encouraged to stay alert, which is probably a good thing.

*

Here's a point that has just occurred to me, and which has absolutely nothing to do with trolleys. When you watch top class golf on the box, the players frequently use a 3 wood off the tee rather than a driver, on the grounds that, although it doesn't propel the ball as far, it is more accurate. Whereas at club level the average golfer can't wait to use "the big stick" at every opportunity. Is there a lesson in this for us cerebral sportsmen?

Which reminds me... One of the great authorities (whose name I have forgotten) once said that eighty percent of golfers should never even carry a driver in their bag. By now you, O reader, should have been playing for long enough to have some idea of what he was getting at. Mull it over....

All I would add is this: ask yourself how much of the trouble you get into on the golf course is due to your driver. If the answer is "Most of it", then bear in mind that there is respectable provenance behind the suggestion that one should throw away one's big stick and never use anything larger than a 3 wood.

Chapter 17

THE NEXT STEP

Let us suppose that you are now in your second year as a practising golfer. It could be the case that, like the golden eagle chick that has for some weeks been flapping its wings while crouched on the edge of its eyrie, perched high up on a cliff, you feel ready to launch yourself into the unknown.

Not entirely unknown, since you will have guides to direct you at every stage, as indeed has the chick, in the shape of its parents. So, what do you do? First, you seek a friend who has a handicap (a golf handicap), and sufficient good nature to accompany you on three 18-hole rounds. (Stop Press: I believe that sometime soon 9-hole sessions will qualify for the process I am about to describe).

Let's say that you rack up 115 shots (43 more than a par of 72) on the first occasion, then 112, then 110. Your friend dutifully records your scores, hole by hole, and signs the cards. You sign them too, and inscribe them with the magic formula "For Handicap Purposes."

You drop them through the appropriate letterbox in the clubhouse and in due course the handicap committee will give the matter some thought.

The scores you have submitted suggest that, given a 40-shot advantage, you might tie with a scratch golfer (handicap zero). So are they going to give you a handicap of 40? Alas, no, the maximum allowance for a man is 28 (and for a woman 36, I think).

But the important thing is, you are now officially a golfer, a 28-handicapper, and eligible for competitions! Well done!

Now all you have to do is play better, enter competitions, (the primary process by which handicaps are monitored and adjusted), "put in" more cards, and reduce your handicap to 20 (competent), then to 12 (competitive), then to a single figure (very good indeed), and so on. If you reach +1 or better, you are absolutely brilliant. Get the picture?

*

*

When I was the worst player in the world and had a handicap of 28 (which masked an ability level of about 40), I couldn't wait to start participating in the monthly medal competitions, and this is a policy which I have no hesitation in recommending to the mature beginner who needs to progress rather quicker than a younger student of the game.

Each time I appeared at the first tee, among the hardened regulars who had been good enough to allow me to infiltrate their number, I would identify myself as a particularly ignorant novice. I would ask the others to keep an eye on me and to straighten me out whenever I strayed from the path of righteousness. This seemed to provide a working arrangement which allowed me to be part of the game without driving anyone mad by my incompetence.

The first tee was a lesson in itself. Imagine sixteen or more people assembled and setting off in groups of three or four. That's a considerable gallery for a novice. While a striker is striking, silence rules; otherwise there is quite a lot of jocularity. Some people respond well to an audience – others don't. For the shrinking violet the badinage can be nerve-racking, the silence petrifying.

There you have it. This is something that one must get used to, and the sooner one starts the better. We know (don't we?) that playing a shot correctly requires all one's attention. So say a prayer. Take your time. Withdraw into your private bubble. Exclude the merry throng from your consciousness. Concentrate... and smash the ball down the middle of the fairway!

Thus it was that I found myself participating in what amounted to regular 4-hour tutorials. The dedicated medallist is a stickler for the rules. So I was learning the rules, and the principles behind the rules, and the conventions behind the principles, and the *caveats* influencing the conventions. I was also learning the error of my ways, whenever my ways deviated from the straight and narrow.

"Hit wrong ball – two shot penalty!" How well I remember that knell of doom ringing out. And even now, looking back on the incident, I have a strong suspicion that the party concerned knew damned well that I was about to strike his ball, and kept it to himself until I had done so! Strict disciplinarians – they make you suffer for your own good.

I learned where not to stand when a player is playing a shot, when not to move on the green, when not to talk, when to replace my ball with a marker, when not to, and the meaning of the phrase "Putt it or mark it." I also learned the rudiments of scoring and the need to score accurately (because one is scoring somebody else's card, and someone else is not happy if one gets it wrong) and how to fill in and sign a card in the right place.

The more one learns, the less dense becomes the fog that obscures one's vision, which increases one's chance of doing the right thing at the appropriate time, which helps one to play better. I owe a considerable debt of gratitude to the dozen or more players who took it in turn to drill the basics into my sometimes not very receptive skull. Such people are part of golf's fabric. Seek them out and you too will enjoy the benefit of their attentions.

Chapter 18

THE SEARCH FOR PERFECTION

Time passes, and there you are, still a 28 handicapper, but now and then hitting some wonderful shots, feeling fitter than you have done for twenty-five years, and enjoying a social life that has never been so active – all thanks to golf.

For most people the game at this level provides more than they had ever hoped for when they first took up the challenge, and they are quite content to surf into the sunset on a wave of contentment. They have my blessing.

However, there are those who always find something to complain about, and this I know full well, for I am one of them. The complaint runs as follows:
"If everything in the garden is so rosy, and if I keep on hitting these wonderful shots, which I do, why is my handicap still 28?"

"Because, although you regularly hit fairway woods that Tiger would be proud of, and flop shots reminiscent of Mickelson, you never complete 18 holes in less than 110 shots. Granted that the par at your course is 72, that suggests that a rating of 28 is in fact flattering you. Your real position in the scheme of things is on a 38 handicap mark (if such a thing existed), which puts you right off the dial on the wrong side."

"Why on earth is this so…?"

"Because, in addition to your good shots, you are also hitting some fair ones, some ordinary ones, some moderate ones and some stinkers."

"Must every shot be good, if I am to improve my standing?"

"By no means. Keep your good shots, keep your fair shots, and your ordinary ones and your moderate ones. The only ones that need to be eliminated are your stinkers."

How do I define a stinker? It is the shot that goes vilely wrong when there is no excuse for it to go vilely wrong, the shot that goes vilely wrong because the player has momentarily taken leave of his senses. In addition, the stinker is the mistake which gets you into such deep trouble that you find yourself wasting several more shots extricating yourself.

At this point I tell the plaintiff of the time, early in my golfing career, when I had completed 17 holes in 91 shots, and was feeling pleased with myself. That complacency was almost certainly the reason I put my third shot at the par-5 18th into a deep greenside bunker.

This was the moment when lunacy took over. From an impossible position in a corner and under an overhang, I persisted in aiming at the flag. If I had chosen the obvious escape route, a sideways exit, I could well have completed the hole in a perfectly reasonable 7. The 14 shots which the 18th hole finally cost me turned a round which might have caused the handicap committee to look upon me with respect into one which provided them with nothing but the gift of laughter.

So, what are the facts of life in this regard?

First the good news. Let us suppose that, from time to time, you have shown that you are capable of completing every hole on your home course in one shot more than par. In other words, you are capable of doing the par fives in six, the par fours in five, the par threes in four. That means you regularly (but alas not invariably) show that you are in need of one extra shot per hole over 18 holes, which is the equivalent of a handicap of 18, which is respectable.

This is a fair reflection of your potential. The fact is that a very ordinary player can easily complete a par five in six shots, even if three of those shots are moderate, <u>provided that all the shots stay on the fairway, and keep going in roughly the right direction, and achieve at least two-thirds of the distance you normally achieve with a reasonably good shot</u>. Is that asking too much? Not at all! That's why I said that, in order to reduce your handicap, all you have to get rid of are the stinkers, the shots which turn a 7 into a 14.

Believe me – I've been there. In fact I am still there at this very moment, as I type this message of hope. I now play off 20, and it is only my addiction to at least two stinkers per round that prevents me from enjoying the kudos that comes with an 18 handicap.

How does one achieve the break-through? What little I know I am happy to share.

The obvious way of getting <u>into</u> trouble is to try to hit the ball too hard. This happens, more often than not, when one steps on to the tee brandishing one's driver. Something about the circumstances appeals to the beast in one, and madness ensues. And of course with a driver one can do more damage to oneself than with any other club.

The way to salvation is to use one's driver sparingly, and only in situations where wide open spaces predominate and hazards are few and far between. In those circumstances there is more chance of getting away with an error, if it should occur.

One is also more likely to find the way to salvation if one constantly reminds oneself that, when swinging the bigger clubs, GOOD contact is far more important than VIOLENT contact.

The other way of getting into trouble is complacency. I know it well – I suffer from it all the time. You start a round muttering "Preparation! Preparation! Preparation!" and you go through the simple and brief process of assessing each shot with the zeal of a bloodhound scenting haggis.

You hit four or five good shots in succession and immediately you tell yourself that you have finally cracked it! Hurrah! You do a little dance. Your concentration evaporates, and is replaced by euphoria. You waltz up to your ball, mentally consigning the greater part of your preparation to the container labelled "No Longer Wanted on Voyage".

Result: you fire the ball into the nearest wood, where it nestles in the sinuosities of a rooting system, out of which you winkle it with the blunt end of your putter with such violence that it crosses the fairway and drowns in a pond. And there you are – well on the way to a 14!

Never mind the profusion of your brilliant shots, three such mistakes will add 21 to your score, and your membership of the 28 Handicap Club will be automatically renewed.

The fact is that, if you drop your guard, you are dead meat. Between shots you can relax, but you cannot afford to get euphoric, and when you "go back to work" you simply must accept that you are entering a war zone.

You must never forget that one good shot is meaningless on its own. Likewise, one good hole is worthless until the other 17 holes have made a sufficient contribution to enable the round to be respectable. One good hole, several good holes, a lot of good holes – all worthless, unless and until the whole shebang is completed without those few total disasters which make so much difference.

If you make use of the last eight paragraphs, you will be particularly careful with regard to your driver, and you will maintain an intense concentration over every shot in a round of 18 holes, irrespective of how well, or how badly you are playing.

It is not a huge burden. One way or another, you are going to play every shot – so why not take your time, apply yourself, and do the job properly? In this way, stinking bad shots will gradually become a thing of the past.

Incidentally, I do think it helps to relax between shots. Sometimes I will prepare a shot correctly and it will come off. "I'm free!" I cry. "Hello, birds, hello trees, hello sky, hello people! I'm free!" If I am going about my business in a proper fashion (which, alas, is not always the case), I also gently exercise my head, neck and shoulders, because that is where tension creeps up on the unsuspecting player. And I "get my breathing right."

A minute or two later I spy my ball, and as I approach it I mutter "Back to the coal face" and the silly smile is replaced by the mask of concentration. Am I making sense?

Chapter 19

MORE OF THE SAME

My next suggestion as regards improving one's handicap finds me trespassing on territory which rightly belongs to your professional advisers. Check it out with them before taking my word for it.

You will find in your early days that whenever you reach a green you are fairly happy to take two putts to get to the hole and a third to sink the ball.

Consider the possibility that the job should be possible in two putts instead of three. Work on it. Let the prospect of saving a shot a hole be your guiding star, and you will find that it can be done. And if you practice, you will find that it can be done more often than you think. There is a saying, in good standing among golf's intelligentsia, which goes, "A man who can putt is a match for anyone." It's probably true. It is based on the premise that anyone can become a good putter, if they work at it. It doesn't mean holing every first putt, however long. It means getting close with every first putt, however long.

You might like to bear in mind another area in which it is possible for relatively ordinary golfers to improve their form by practice.

I have often heard it said that so-and-so is "deadly from a hundred yards out." This means he/she has spent time practicing approach shots (the aerial "pitch" with the most lofted irons, and the less elevated bouncy-bouncy "chip and run" with the 7, 8, 9 irons), with a view to getting the ball fairly close to the hole in one shot, from up to a hundred yards out. It is definitely a department of the game that rewards those who work at it, and it doesn't require huge talent or extraordinary strength.

Now here is a lesson in stupidity which will save you five years, if you take it to heart. I spent five years assiduously working on my short game by practising pitches, and my approach to greens consisted of nothing else. The end result was unsatisfactory – one in ten turned out useful, the rest were rubbish.

After five years I reviewed the situation by collating the advice given on this subject by three of the game's greatest professors – Harvey Penick, Tommy Armour and Bobby Jones. On one topic they were unanimous – only "pitch" if there is an obstacle between you and the hole – on all other occasions chip and run.

This advice was given because "pitching" is much more difficult than "chipping." I had been aware of this advice for five years, but for some reason I thought it didn't apply to me. After five years I came to my senses and did as I was told – and the improvement was instantaneous and significant.

*

On the morning of Saturday 3rd December 2005 I experienced a revelation. It was then that I finally put my finger on perhaps the main reason why so many amateur, social, part-time golfers (people like me) do not improve their handicaps as much as they should.

The basic facts are as follows: most games of golf played at club level are either Matchplay or Stableford. In Matchplay winning holes is what counts, not the number of shots you take over 18 holes. In Stableford, your score is the total of the points you earn at the holes that you play well. Your bad holes are of no consequence.

The alternative is Strokeplay, in which the only number that matters is the number of shots you require to complete 18 holes. Virtually all professional golf is Strokeplay. However it is a less prevalent in normal club golf.

What difference does it make?

In Matchplay or Stableford, if you are winning the hole easily, you relax and take three putts instead of one, because it doesn't matter, or the opposition concedes and you don't putt at all.

Likewise, if you are losing a hole easily, you will lose interest, write off the hole in your own mind, play bad shots without worrying. You are already thinking of a new start at the next tee.

You may win your Matchplay, or your Stableford, but you will have spent three or four hours in an environment where, quite frequently, hitting bad shots doesn't matter. Over a period of time this acceptance of poor shots, played with inadequate preparation and concentration, will make you careless, and limit your chance of ever getting down to a respectable handicap, even though your best game is quite good enough to achieve that goal.

To improve, you have to maintain concentration over every shot you play over 18 holes. Matchplay and Stableford encourage you to drop your guard far too often for your own good.

What's to be done?

Play whatever sort of game the occasion demands, but let a part of your mind be counting every shot, and reminding you that the total you rack up over 18 holes is what really matters, not the number of holes you win, or, in Stableford, the points you accumulate on your "good" holes.

Some people write down their score on each hole. Alternatively, it is possible to keep a score in one's head, by taking 5 as your target score for each hole – 5 times 18 equals 90 (which is 18 over a par of 72, for example, and therefore respectable). If you do the first hole in 6, you are "1 over". If you do the second in 5, you are still "1 over". Complete the third in three and your score becomes "1 under". An 8 at the fourth sends your score soaring up to "2 over". And so it goes on. If your score is "7 over fives" after 18 holes, you have gone round in 97. The mathematics are simple, you don't have to write anything down, and it keeps you in touch with the most important number.

Some people don't have to keep a score. They simply make it a rule that they only address their ball if they are going to give it 100%. Every shot counts.

The situation is not as grim as I may have made it sound. The fact is that, if you are going to play a shot, the difference between 100% and casual is just a little more time, just a little more thought, just a little more concentration. It makes sense, feels good and costs nothing. The alternative is to play in a way that encourages you to get worse rather than better. Who needs that?

Chapter 20

Putt-putt

As you are aware, it has been my intention to avoid any attempt to teach the reader how to actually play the game. Apart from advocating the long swing, I am no more than the Gunga Din of the golf course, the water-carrier, the purveyor of sweetmeats and field-dressings for the thirsty, the hungry, the wounded and the sick at heart.

Partly this is because no one is more alive to my incompetence than I am. Partly it is because the Royal and Ancient Golf Club (the supreme authority for the game in Europe) advised me not to. "If your slim volume amounts to a teaching manual, based on your alleged expertise," said a spokeswoman, "your amateur status might be in jeopardy."

"Heaven forbid!" I replied.

That was then, and this is now. Then I had nothing. Now I have the secret of the alchemist's stone. We're talking about alchemy at its lowest conceivable level, but even so it is not to be sneered at.

I know how to turn really hopeless putters into much less hopeless hopeless putters. I was the former, now I am the latter, thanks to an approach which I suspect is original – I certainly haven't come across anything like it in my extensive reading on the subject.

From my perspective, helping the hopeless is something that one must do, irrespective of the consequences to one's amateur status. Gunga Din would agree.

This is how it's done.

You go through your routine as usual, and line up the putt to your satisfaction, choosing a line by taking into account distance, slopes and cambers, and whatever else is relevant. Then hold the address position with the clubhead hanging two or three inches behind the ball.

Now, without moving anything else, move your right foot forward an inch. You will find that your set-up is now lining up the ball along a line that deviates from your original choice by about a foot – towards the left hand side. Line up on something while in that position. A leaf, a patch of yellow grass, a worm cast, a distant tree trunk.

Then move your right foot back two inches, and do the same to the right of the hole. Carefully. Then return to your original position, take aim and pull the trigger.

I am persuaded that creating two points of reference, one to the left and one to the right of the target, improves your chance of being on your chosen line when you finally hit the ball.

Try it – it only takes an extra few seconds. If it doesn't work for you, so what? After all, this advice is of dubious provenance (what do I know?), and is for really hopeless putters only. It won't have done you any harm.

(Two years later)
I am still happy with the suggestion that appears above, but here's a more down-to-earth approach to putting. All golf balls have brand names and coded specifications printed on them. This amounts to a variety of lines (some straight, some curved).

Let's say that you make a habit of "marking" your ball on the green. You squat down, place your marker, pick up your ball and clean it.

As you replace it, you ensure that there is a straight line of letters or figures on the upper surface of the ball. Take a few seconds to ensure that that line is pointing in the direction you have chosen for your line of putt.

Then you stand up, glance at the hole, glance down at the "arrow" on the ball. This the interesting bit: sometimes you find that it is pointing in the direction of your choice, sometimes it is slightly off line. Why this should be I have yet to work out. If you like the signal it is giving you, hit along that line. If not, use the line as a basis for a deliberate deviation.

What's the point? The point is that as you strike the ball you are actually looking at an "arrow" and you know where it is heading.

Without this aid, you can do as much preparation as you like, but when you strike the ball you will be following a line which is no more than a memory of the last time you looked in the direction of your target. That can be quite disconcerting, whereas having a signpost to look at as you actually strike is reassuring. Elderly novices need all the reassurance they can get.

(PS. Incidentally, I tend to use the "points of reference" for shorter putts, and the ball decorations for the longer ones.

Irrespective of my loony theories, it really does make sense to mark and clean your ball on the green, and to wipe your putter head. One blade of grass, or drop of moisture, or spot of mud, attached to either ball or putter, can undo the best-laid plans, and the best-played shots. Besides, bending and/or squatting is good for you.)

Chapter 21

CONCLUSION

You now know everything that I know. However there is plenty more to learn. Speaking for myself, it is my firm intention to fill in the many gaps in my knowledge of the Great Game, because I have a keen appetite for more and more information on any subject that I find interesting.

Some of you may be similarly inquisitive. If so, you won't have to seek out avenues that invite exploration. They will tap you on the shoulder at times of their own choosing.

Over a period, you will hear tales of heroic feats achieved on very special courses, and there will be a stirring in the soul, a burning desire to visit these legendary battlefields and take up the challenge which they represent.

I have a postcard of the first tee at Machrihanish, which looks extremely beautiful and extremely alarming at the same time. It requires a bold strike across open sea – part of the open sea between the West of Scotland and Northern Ireland, I am informed. One day I will go there…. and feel my knees trembling.

I have a first edition of "Stalky and Co" by Rudyard Kipling, a fictionalised account of his schooldays at the Imperial Service College, Westward Ho! Inside the front cover is a cutting from a 1927 newspaper, in which J. H. Taylor, three times Open Golf Champion, reminisces about his boyhood, caddie-ing for the schoolmasters who feature in the book. The school is long gone, as is Kipling, as is Taylor, as are the schoolmasters, but the golf club in question, North Devon, is still there, hard by the Pebbleridge, where the boys used to bathe in the Atlantic when Victoria was queen. One day I shall go and play there. Maybe paddle in the Atlantic.

[Two years later: I have been there: it is the rough and rugged Mother and Father of all Links courses. I played very badly in a strong wind and loved every moment of it. I didn't have the opportunity to paddle, which is an extra reason for a second visit.]

Talking of Kipling, the literature that golf has inspired is extensive, much of it fascinating. P.G. Wodehouse, Bernard Darwin, Henry Longhurst, Ian Fleming, Patrick Campbell, John Betjeman and John Updike (to name just a few) have put their love of the game on paper, and offer the reader the chance to share the thrills and spills, without the necessity of leaving the fireside.

134

Or.... or you may become intrigued by golf's physical impact on the landscape, and eventually the day may dawn when you find yourself asking, "Who designed this course? And wasn't he a clever devil to put a bunker just where it can be most annoying? And aren't those trees majestic?" That's when one first encounters great names: Colt, Abercrombie, Fowler, Croome, Mackenzie, Hutchinson and Simpson (no relation) – just some of the designers who, a hundred years ago and more, prepared the terrain which we are now privileged to enjoy in its magnificent maturity. And for some of us this creates an irresistible desire to know more about these heroes and their work.

Let us not forget the urge that drives some golfers to discover foreign fields. Wherever they go, they find an environment which is friendly, surroundings which are familiar, and foreigners with whom they have something in common. What better introduction to someone else's country and culture could one hope for?

The permutations, the opportunities, the attractions are endless. As I think I have already mentioned, golf is not just a game. It is a passport to Utopia – to life as it should be.

But do not despair, those of you who have no interest in strange courses, dusty books, landscape gardening, and foreign travel. These are optional extras. The essence of the magic is out there, where the breezes blow, when you plant your tee, balance your ball, flourish your club, favour the far distance with a look of calculated defiance, then sink imperceptibly into the position of address.